)seph L. Breeden

Living with CECL:

Mortgage
Modeling Alternatives

May 2018

ISBN 978-1-7321696-0-9
©2018 by Prescient Models LLC
email: info@prescientmodels.com
website: www.prescientmodels.com

Acknowledgements

The author would like to thank the sponsors of the Deep Future Analytics CECL Mortgage Study: Allied Solutions, NAFCU – National Association of Federally-Insured Credit Unions, and OnApproach. The support and encouragement of these organizations made this study possible. The Deep Future Analytics CECL Mortgage Study was initiated to answer important questions about how to apply the rules of CECL to term loans. Prescient Models is a partner of DFA and provided the technology for the study. The author served as the principle investigator for the study.

Any opinions expressed here are solely those of the author and may not represent the opinions of the sponsors.

The author would also like to thank Maxim Vaskouski, PhD for performing the heavy lifting on the data analysis and Eugenia Leonova, PhD for additional support. In addition, the analysis relied on the tremendous contributions of a great team of scientists: Aleh Yablonski, PhD; Anna Glaz, PhD; Denis Vylegzhanin, PhD; and Veronika Tulyeva. Thank you, all.

This book benefitted greatly for the keen eyes and pointed suggestions of Rhonda Black at Prescient Models LLC and Lisa Bucki at 1x1 Media, LLC (www.1x1media.com).

About the Author

Joseph L. Breeden, *PhD CEO, Prescient Models LLC*

Dr. Breeden has been designing and deploying credit risk models for loan portfolios since 1996. His expertise includes scoring, forecasting, stress testing, and economic capital models. Since 2011, Dr. Breeden has been CEO of Prescient Models, where he leads a consulting and product development team in this space, focusing on loan-level models for forecasting, stress testing, and pricing.

Dr. Breeden has applied similar analytical techniques to the price of fine wines. The forecasts created on a database of 1.5 million auction prices are available at auctionforecast.com.

Previously, Dr. Breeden co-founded Strategic Analytics in 1999, where he led the design of advanced analytic solutions including the invention of Dual-time Dynamics. He has created models through the 1995 Mexican Peso Crisis, the 1997 Asian Economic Crisis, the 2001 Global Recession, the 2003 Hong Kong SARS Recession, and the 2007-2009 US Mortgage Crisis and Global Financial Crisis. These crises have provided him with a rare perspective on crisis management and the analytics needs of executives for strategic decision-making.

Dr. Breeden has published over 40 academic articles, a dozen trade publications, and six patents. His book *Reinventing Retail Lending Analytics: Forecasting, Stress Testing, Capital, and Scoring for a World of Crises* was first published by Riskbooks in 2010 and is currently in its second edition.

Dr. Breeden received separate BS degrees in mathematics and physics in 1987 from Indiana University. He earned a Ph.D. in physics in 1991 from the University of Illinois studying real-world applications of chaos theory, nonlinear dynamics, and genetic algorithms, particularly in the areas of data analysis and astrophysics.

The rest of his resume can be found at www.josephlbreeden.com.

Contents

Preface

We developed the Living with CECL series to provide useful information for practitioners who are trying to adapt to and comply with the new accounting rules for Current Expected Credit Loss (CECL).

Mortgage Modeling Alternatives is the first of the series and contains many technical details that will be referred back to in later volumes. This book seeks to disclose as many modeling details, results, and validation tests as possible so as to provide a reference for comparison and best practices.

The book is organized into three parts. Part I: Study Summary provides an overview of CECL, the design of the mortgage study, and the key comparative results across the models tested. Part II: Model Details provides in-depth discussions of how the models were designed and estimated, the coefficients, and the validation. Part III: Background provides additional conceptual material. Chapters 11 and 12 may be particularly useful to those new to modeling, and Chapter 13 puts CECL modeling in the context of lending analytics overall. A version of Chapter 13 appeared in RMA Journal Breeden (2017b)

PART I

Study Summary

Introduction to the Study

1.1 Overview

The release of the new rules for loan loss reserves accounting by the Financial Accounting Standards Board (FASB) will bring many changes in the lending industry and no small amount of uncertainty about how to comply with the new guidelines. The Current Expected Credit Loss (CECL) framework seeks to apply forward-looking methods to estimate credit losses for setting loss reserves. This represents a dramatic departure from traditional methods of estimating the Allowance for Loan and Lease Losses (ALLL) that relied upon averages of historic losses.

These changes were obviously necessary following the US Mortgage Crisis of 2009. Figure 1.1 compares loss reserves to the forward-looking 12 months of losses (annual charge-off rate) from FDIC data on the banking industry FDIC If under the previous rules loss reserves were intended to cover the next 12 months of losses, clearly this did not happen. Loss reserves barely registered the 2001 recession and did not peak until a year after the 2009 recession. In all cases, reserves can be seen to be too low entering a recession and too high afterward, because the reserves were backward-looking to the previous phase of the economy. Reserves estimated under CECL will still not be perfect, because no one has a perfect view of the future of the economy, but the loss reserve estimates can be much better.

The final guidance from FASB (FASB 2016) indicates that financial institutions may use different estimation methods for CECL depending upon the size and sophistication of the institution. This flexibility brings benefits to the institutions, but it will also bring a significant amount of confusion. Under the published guidance, all institutions will need new models to satisfy the rules, even if those models are simplistic for

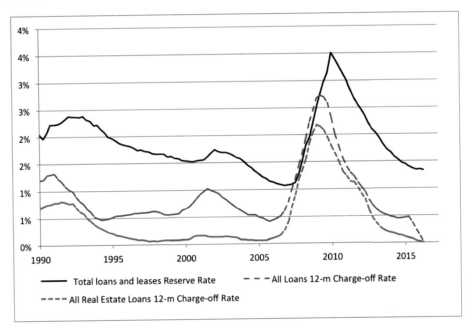

Figure 1.1. A comparison of industry loan and lease loss reserves to forward-looking 12-month cumulative actual losses for all loans and just real estate loans. Data from FDIC.

the smaller institutions. Institutions will need to determine for themselves how much sophistication they need or want. An even greater problem may come from examiners, auditors, and validators trying to review these models. They will also be trying to gauge how much sophistication the lender should have employed.

1.2 Study Goals

The primary goal of the Deep Future Analytics CECL Mortgage Alternatives Study was to create a public document that all parties can use as a reference to the strengths and weakness of the available techniques. This assessment will not be a search for the "best" answer. Rather, we want to assess the range of answers produced by different techniques in the context of accuracy, complexity, and stability for portfolios of different sizes. Of course, modelers, validators, and examiners will continue to debate what is appropriate, but practitioners may leverage this study as a clear data point on an important asset class.

Note that the study results presented here are revised and expanded from those provided previously in "The Deep Future Analytics CECL Study: Alternatives, Impacts, Accuracy, and Complexity" (Breeden 2017a). Among the changes were the inclusion of seasonality in the models and providing additional tests.

1.3 Study Design

This study analyzed large datasets from Fannie Mae and Freddie Mac on conforming mortgage performance. The same data was modeled by the most commonly employed loss forecasting techniques within the context of the final CECL rules.

The study included a comparison of the level and timing of the predicted loss reserves through the last recession, model accuracy tests, stability of the techniques as the size of the dataset is reduced, and an assessment of the implementation complexity.

The greatest advantage of this study is the consistency of model creation across the various techniques tested. The same dataset spanning the same time frame with the same segmentation was employed throughout. The same economic scenarios were used for all models.

The Results Summary in Chapter 2 provides a quick comparison of the results from the various modeling techniques, but complete details are given for each model type in later chapters. Our goal is complete disclosure for all models, so that institutions may judge for themselves how the models were created and the reasonableness of the test results.

1.4 Current Expected Credit Losses (CECL)

CECL was developed concurrently with IFRS 9. IFRS 9 is the new accounting standard from the International Accounting Standards Board (IASB) also with the intent of creating forward-looking loss reserves. Rather than follow IFRS 9, FASB elected to use lifetime loss estimation for all loans rather than having a multi-stage approach. This decision was to simplify the process for the thousands of smaller lenders in the US. The stated goals of lifetime loss estimation and using current economic conditions for the near-term and relaxing onto the long-run economic conditions for the rest of the forecast naturally lead to the same kind of models being discussed for IFRS 9. However, in an attempt to soften the burden for smaller institutions, the CECL guidelines state explicitly that complex models are not required for smaller institutions. Nevertheless, finding a simpler approach that does not carry a harsh penalty in loss reserve levels or in auditor and examiner review is not obvious.

The CECL guidelines provide the following principles that should be considered when estimating losses.

1.4.1 Forseeable future

CECL distinguishes between the foreseeable and unforeseeable future, Figure 1.2. For 30-year mortgages being considered in this study, no one can create reliable macroeconomic projections 30 years forward. Instead, most practitioners consider the "foreseeable" future for the economy to be on the order of 24 months. Beyond this near future, the only plausible economic scenario is to use a through-the-cycle (TTC) average.

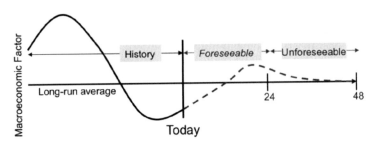

Figure 1.2. A visualization of a mean-reverting process transitioning between the near-term "foreseeable" future and the long-term "unforseeable" future.

For the model types tested here, a single model is used to span the entire forecast horizon, but mean-reverting macroeconomic scenarios are created as described in Chapter 10 so as to create a smooth transition between the foreseeable and unforeseeable periods.

Certainly many practitioners will create two models, one for the near term with a baseline macroeconomic scenario, and one for the remaining lifetime behavior with a TTC macroeconomic scenario. The challenge with having a separate TTC model is that many analysts will try to use just a historic average loss rate, but such loss rates are averages of previous portfolios, not necessarily the current portfolio. The single-model approach of modifying the inputs has the advantage of basing the full lifetime forecast on the current portfolio. Also, only one model will need to be validated, rather than two.

1.4.2 Lifetime loss estimation

The next big change in CECL is the adoption of loss reserves for the full lifetime of the loans rather than just the next 12 months. This will cause some headaches in the transition from old rules to new, but the concept is good. It should make the loss reserves less volatile through the economic cycle and provides lenders with valuable information for pricing loans.

"Lifetime loss" is measured from the present age of the loan to it furthest non-cancellable end point. For fixed term loans, this is easily determined. Lines-of-credit or renewable loans are more complex, and will be discussed in Section 2.10.2.

Reserving for lifetime losses means the remaining life of the loan. Ideally, for a loan of any age, we would like to compute the expected loss for the remaining life until termination. The natural and most well-known method for accomplishing this is vintage analysis. However, vintage analysis is not well known at smaller institutions, so the final CECL rules stated explicitly that vintage analysis is not required. The models employed in this study all manage to create a remaining life of loan estimation, though only a few explicitly use lifecycles versus age of the loan as is done in vintage analysis, Figure 1.3.

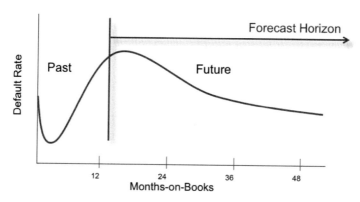

Figure 1.3. Illustration of reserving for the remaining life of a loan.

The examples in the CECL rules also imply that one consequence of not using some form of age-of-loan analysis could be that the same lifetime loss amount is held for the life of the loan regardless of its age. We explore the consequences of such an approach in the Historic Precedent model in Section 9.1, which was modeled as closely as possible on the first example in the final CECL guidelines.

1.4.3 Discounting

The CECL guidelines recognize that in a lifetime loss calculation, losses or revenue in the distant future are not as important as in the near-term, under a time-value-of-money concept. Discounting is given as an option, but one that may potentially reduce the level of loss reserves.

Direct loss discounting

From a theoretical perspective, we could look at discounting from two ways. CECL is about loss forecasting. If we have a model that predicts the monthly (or quarterly) expected loss through the life of the loan, that loss stream could be discounted directly in order to adjust for the difference between near-term and far-future losses. That adjustment would be done using the effective interest rate on the loan. Although the effective interest includes any premiums or discounts in the loan origination or servicing, none of that information is available in the present study. Therefore, the origination interest rate on the mortgage is used throughout as the effective interest rate.

If a model is used to compute the expected loss amount each month, then the formula for computing the discounted loss is given in Equation 1.1.

$$\text{Discounted Lifetime Loss} = \sum_{t=1}^{N} \frac{\text{Loss}(t)}{(1 + r_{\text{eff}}/12)^{t-1}} \tag{1.1}$$

where r_{eff} is the effective annual interest rate of the loan, N is the number of months in the forecast horizon, and $\text{Loss}(t)$ is the expected loss amount predicted for a specific month. Any model that produces estimates at intervals may be discounted.

Discounted cash flows

Discounted cash flows (DCF) is a standard technique in finance for considering the time value of money and is mentioned explicitly in the CECL guidelines. Unlike the loss discounting above, DCF assumes that predictions of periodic (monthly or quarterly) principal and interest payments are discounted and used in a net present value calculation.

$$\text{DCF Loss} = \text{Outstanding Balance}(0) - PV \tag{1.2}$$

where Outstanding Balance(0) is the balance at the beginning of the forecast. PV is the present value of future cash flows, computed as

$$PV = \sum_{t=1}^{N} \frac{\text{Total Payments}(t)}{(1 + r_{\text{eff}}/12)^{t-1}} \qquad (1.3)$$

For the current study, Total Payments(i) is assumed to be

$$\begin{aligned}
\text{Total Payments}(t) = &\text{Expected principal Payment}(t) \\
&+ \text{Expected Interest Payment}(t) \qquad (1.4) \\
&+ \text{Expected Recoveries}(t)
\end{aligned}$$

Equation 1.4 does not include late fees or other penalty fees, which is common practice in mortgage DCF calculations. However, DCF models of products like credit card will probably need to include late fees since they are a large fraction of the revenue stream.

For a fixed term loan, the scheduled principal and interest payments are known from the standard amortization formulas.

$$\text{Scheduled Payment}(t) = B\frac{r(1-r)^n}{((1+r)^n - 1)} \qquad (1.5)$$

$$\text{Scheduled Interest Payment}(t) = B\frac{r(1+r)^n - (1+r)^t}{((1+r)^n - 1)} \qquad (1.6)$$

where B is the original loan amount.

$$\begin{aligned}
\text{Scheduled Principal Payment}(t) = &\text{ Scheduled Payment}(t) \\
&-\text{Interest Payment}(t)
\end{aligned}$$

To get the expected payments for Equation 1.4, the scheduled payments must be adjusted for the possibility that the loan either default or prepays, either of which will reduce the probability of receiving the full payment stream. Those adjustments will be dependent upon the model chosen.

Although DCF is common practice, not all lifetime loss estimates may produce monthly loss values suitable for created the estimated payments required. To accommodate such situations, the CECL guidelines again state that discounted cash flows are not required. However, without DCF the lifetime loss reserves may be higher than with DCF.

1.4.4 Aggregate or loan-level

Comments from FASB about CECL modeling have stated more or less directly that modeling is to be done in aggregate for loans that are sufficiently similar and loan-level modeling is only to be done for unique loans. These comments often appear to be a mandate for aggregate models, such as vintage models. If true, we believe that this position will evolve.

As we will discuss in Chapter 13, large institutions with CCAR (Comprehensive Capital Analysis and Review) models are hoping to apply them for CECL by modifying only the macroeconomic scenarios and exposure at default calculations. Since regulators has been pushing CCAR institutions to develop loan-level models, we consider it highly unlikely that FASB would reject loan-level models.

Loan-level methods are invariably more complex, which will weigh in the model selection process for some lenders, but they naturally provide supplementary business value in account pricing and management. Therefore, this study considers aggregate and loan-level methods equally.

1.5 Modeling Approaches

The final CECL guidance provides a list of techniques that may be used for estimating loss reserves. Rather than being a list from which practitioners should choose, the list makes clear a philosophy that any approach is allowed as long as it adheres to the principles of the guidance and is appropriate for the size and complexity of the institution. To illustrate the range of possible options, FASB provided a list of candidate methods:

- Discounted cash flow analysis
- Average charge-off method (sometimes referred to as "loss rate")
- Vintage analysis
- Static pool analysis
- Roll rate method (Migration analysis)
- Probability of default method
- Regression analysis

The Federal Reserve has previously provided documents (Reserve 2013) on methods appropriate for CCAR modeling that partially overlap this list, but are far from identical. This is notable since the largest institutions intend to use their CCAR models for CECL and the Fed, OCC, FDIC, and NCUA will have examination roles relative to CECL. In many respects, CECL may just be a stress test model run with a mean-reverting baseline scenario, so the Fed's recommendations are also worth consideration. Lastly, we have the academic literature on portfolio forecasting and stress testing that is both much broader and also rather more precise in its language about defining models. The FASB list of modeling methods goes largely undefined in the guidelines. In providing definitions, we need to recognize that they are not all comparable. The challenge is to define what a model is. All of the above are intended to be statistical models in some sense, not purely algebraic expressions, so they should include parameters estimated from the data. The creation of these parameters (aka coefficients) requires an estimation algorithm. Therefore, a modeling methodology is equation(s) plus coefficient(s) plus estimator(s). Looking again at that the list from the guidelines, average charge-off method, roll-rate method, migration analysis (actually a distinct approach) and probability of default (PD) method are all systems of equations, each with coefficients to be estimated, somehow. None of these terms defines a complete modeling approach. Vintage analysis indexVintage and static pool analysis refer to data structures, namely vintage time series by segment. They may be used with any of a wide range of equations and with various estimators. Some commentators

The alternative to vintage is simple time series. A time series approach is implied but not required with roll rate models. Loan-level modeling is another option, which the guidelines might have meant by regression analysis. Regression analysis is actually an estimation technique that may be used with any of the above systems of equations or data structures. Lastly, discounted cash flows are a true anomaly. They are a system of equations which rely on some other modeling technique to estimate the expected payment streams adjusted for the possibility of charge-off or early pay-off. Therefore, any of the other methods on the list may serve as inputs to the discounted cash flows approach. We could instead think of DCF as an aggregation method rather than a modeling technique. So in reviewing the list above, none of the items represent a complete modeling methodology. Further, many of the best estimation techniques are not listed and loan-level modeling is not clearly stated. Therefore, creating a modeling methodology for CECL requires looking beyond the quite heterogeneous list found there. The correct process for loss estimation involves three steps:

1. What variables will be predicted, e.g. roll rates, PD, etc.?
2. What level will they be modeled, e.g. aggregate time series, vintage series, or loan-level?
3. What estimator will be used?

Only the last question has clear best practices from the academic literature. The first two choices depend upon the available data and analyst expertise.

To choose the set of models for the study, let's first begin by defining the full range of options. The systems of equations one might employ includes:

- Default and Prepayment Rates
- Roll Rates and Prepayment Rate
- Grade Migration
- State Transition
- Basel II: PD, EAD, LGD, & PA

In the list above, lifetime loss modeling always requires some form of prepayment estimation, so all of the systems include this either explicitly or implicitly. Default and prepayment refer to modeling monthly balance rates. Roll rates have a classic delinquency structure where the balance (or accounts) in one delinquency state are compared to the balance (or accounts) in the previous delinquency state the previous month. Grade migration usually refers to creating states according to credit scores or risk grades and modeling the transition probabilities between them. State transition involves modeling every possible transition from one delinquency state to another, including pay-off and charge-off. PD, EAD, LGD, and PA are probability of default, exposure at default, loss given default, and probability of attrition. PA was added to support lifetime estimation, but the rest were popularized in the Basel II design. Each of these structures may be modified according to the product and business goals.

Any option in the systems of equations above may be modeled at different levels of aggregation. The following terms define the possible data structures.

- Time series
- Vintage aggregate time series
- Loan-level performance

For example, vintage roll rates, loan-level state transitions, and time series grade migrations are all quite common. The Basel II equations can be found modeled at all three levels. In fact, loan-level models may include "vintage affects" by considering the age of the account in the estimation. Given these options and the limitations of the available data, this study uses the models in Table 1.1. The names are those most commonly used, but as explained above they do not capture the full nature of the model.

Name in Study	System of Equations	Data Structure	Estimator
Historic averages	Default and prepayment Rates	Time series	12-month prior average
Time series	Default and prepayment Rates	Time series	Logistic regression
Roll rate	Balance roll rates	Time series	Logistic regression
Vintage	Basel II + attrition	Vintage series	Age-period-cohort (APC)
State transition	State transition	Loan-level	Logistic regression
Discrete time survival	Basel II + attrition	Loan-level	APC + logistic regression

Table 1.1. Models types tested for lifetime loss estimation under CECL.

Each of the methods defined in Table 1.1 above was also used as input to a discounted cash flow calculation, reinforcing the fact that DCF is not a model but rather an aggregation method.

For all of these methods, the end states were default and attrition. Default was taken as 180 days past due. Attrition corresponds to a complete pay-off of the outstanding balance. Any balance dynamics subsequent to default were assumed to be part of the recovery process. Recoveries were assumed to be a constant 70% of losses based upon historic experience. This was done because recovery modeling is a separate problem with its own range of possible approaches. This approach simplifies the problem by removing the need to consider multiple partial charge-offs.

1.5.1 Historic averages

Averages of past history should not really be considered a modeling technique. Historic averages only work if everything is steady state—a constant economy, constant loan growth, and constant origination credit quality. In reality none of these is true, which directly precipitated CECL. Moving averages are included here to provide a comparison of how loan loss reserves have most commonly been computed pre-CECL, thus providing a comparison between old and new practices.

1.5.2 Time series models

The simplest forward-looking model in this study requires creating macroeconomic time series models of the balance default and pay-down rates. Lifetime losses can then be simulated by projecting forward under a mean-reverting base macroeconomic scenario until all currently outstanding balances are either paid or charge off. Transformation of the macroeconomic data and model estimation are primary considerations.

Pure macroeconomic time series models necessarily assume that all portfolio dynamics are explainable by the economy. Since portfolio management actions are typically correlated to economic conditions, this implies that the lender's future underwriting and account management decisions are predictable from macroeconomic scenarios based upon past actions. For the entire lending industry, previous studies suggest this may be true (Breeden and Canals-Cerdá 2016). However, this is a strong assumption for an individual lender.

1.5.3 Roll rate models

For the last 40 years, the two most common kinds of models for retail lending portfolios are credit scores and roll rates. Roll rate models are a kind of state transition model, but estimated on aggregate monthly balance flows from one delinquency bucket to the next.

Historically roll rate models have used moving averages of past rolls. For CECL estimation, the net balance roll rate from one delinquency bucket to the next is modeled with macroeconomic factors. In addition, the balance pay-down rate is modeled with macroeconomic data so that both charge-off and pay-off end states are included. Thus, the roll rate model is like the time series model, but will intermediate delinquency transitions added.

The final lifetime loss is calculated by summing the monthly losses until all existing loans reach zero balance, as described above.

1.5.4 Vintage models

Vintage models naturally capture the timing of losses and attrition versus age of the loan, and therefore are an obvious choice for lifetime loss calculations. An Age-Period-Cohort approach is commonly used to estimate such models. Using rates for probability of default (PD), exposure at default (EAD), loss given default (LGD), and probability of attrition (PA), monthly loss forecasts are created and aggregated to a lifetime loss estimate.

Each key rate is decomposed into a lifecycle function versus the age of the loan, a credit risk function versus origination date (vintage), and an environment function versus calendar date. The lifecycle function captures the timing of losses or attrition. The environment function is an index of sensitivity to macroeconomic changes, which is then correlated to macroeconomic factors as was done with the time series and roll rate models.

Macroeconomic scenarios are used to project the future value of the environment function, which is then combined with the vintage and lifecycle functions to produce monthly forecasts for each vintage. Lifetime loss forecast sum across vintages and calendar date to the end of the loans term or until the outstanding balance reaches zero.

1.5.5 State transition models

State transition models are the loan-level equivalent of roll rate models. Rather than modeling aggregate movements between delinquency states, the probability of transition is computed for each account. The states considered are current, delinquent up to a maximum of six months delinquent, charge-off, and pay-off. Account transition probabilities are modeled rather than the dollar transitions in the roll rate model.

For modeling, a recommended approach would be to create a multinomial regression model from each non-terminal state, predicting all of the other states the account can transition to. The regression model would consider external macroeconomic drivers as well as internal factors for the accounts, such as FICO, loan-to-value (LTV), etc. Functions of age may also be included in order to capture lifecycle effects.

To make forecasts, if the input variables to the transition probability models satisfy the Markov condition of having no memory prior to the current state, then the forecasts may be created via a series of matrix multiplies as in the Markov chain approach. However, if the input factors do have memory, such as number of times delinquent in the previous six months (a common predictive factor), then a Monte Carlo approach must be applied to a sample of the accounts to simulate possible portfolio performance. At each time step each account is assigned a specific state based upon the probability of that transition and a drawn random number.

In all cases the probabilities are functions of time, because the macroeconomic scenarios will change with time using the same mean-reverting scenarios described earlier. The accounts will be simulated until they reach a terminal state such as charge-off or pay-off, or they reach the end of term.

EAD and LGD are modeled separately as functions of the age of the loan to capture balance pay-down with time.

1.5.6 Discrete time survival models

Discrete time survival models are the loan-level enhancement to vintage models, usually with the implication of creating loan-level models with scoring attributes. For the present study, the lifecycle and macroeconomic correlations from the vintage model estimation are used as fixed inputs to a panel data model with scoring attributes. This differs from standard discrete time survival models only in the two step approach where lifecycle and economic sensitivities are estimated first rather than simultaneously. This is done to avoid multicolinearity problems when trying to estimate everything simultaneously. PD, PA, and EAD are estimated with this process.

Separate origination and behavioral models are built, the former using only factors available at origination and the latter using both origination factors and behavioral factors such as recent delinquency. For the behavioral models, the coefficients are a function of forecast horizon, because any delinquent account will have either cured or charged-off within six to twelve months. The remainder of the forecast is thus dominated by persistent factors like FICO score and LTV.

The final lifetime loss forecasts are created by aggregating the loan-level monthly loss estimates.

1.6 Mortgage Data

A combined, publicly available dataset from Fannie Mae and Freddie Mac was used for model creation and assessment. The data provides origination and performance information on conforming 30-year fixed rate mortgages.

In addition to monthly loan status, the database contains a number of attributes suitable for loan-level credit risk estimation. The full list of data fields for Fannie Mae and Freddie Mac appears in Table 1.2.

Origination fields	Performance fields
Loan sequence number	Loan sequence number
Credit score	Monthly reporting period
First payment date	Current actual UPB
First time homebuyer flag	Current loan delinquency status
Maturity date	Loan age
Metropolitan statistical area	Remaining months to legal maturity
Mortgage insurance percentage	Repurchase flag
Number of units	Modification flag
Occupancy status	Zero balance code
CLTV – cumulative loan to value	Zero balance effective date
DTI – debt to income	Current interest rate
Original UPB (unpaid balance)	Current deferred UPB
LTV – loan to value	DOLPI – Date of last paid installment
Original interest rate	Mortgage insurance (MI) recoveries
Channel	Net sales proceeds
PPM flag	Non MI recoveries
Product type	Expenses
Property state	
Property type	
Postal code	
Loan purpose	
Original loan term	
Number of borrowers	
Seller name	
Servicer name	

Table 1.2. Origination and performance data fields available in the Fannie Mae and Freddie Mac datasets.

For the models developed in the study, the following definitions were used:

- Default: current loan delinquency status>=3, i.e. 90+ days past due (DPD)
- Active: non-default and current actual UPB>0

- Attrition: zero balance code=1 (prepaid)
- Outstanding balance: current actual UPB if status = Active
- Default balance: current actual UPB if status = default
- Origination balance: current actual UPB if Current Date = Vintage
- Loss: Default balance + Accrued Interest + Total Costs – Total Proceeds
- Accrued interest: Default balance*((Current Interest Rate/ 100-0.0035)/12)*(Months between Last Principal and Interest Paid Date and Zero Balance Date)
- Total costs: Foreclosure Costs + Property Preservation and Repair Costs + Asset Recovery Costs + Miscellaneous Holding Expenses and Credits + Associated Taxes for Holding Property
- Total proceeds: Net Sales Proceeds + Credit Enhancement Proceeds + Repurchase Make Whole Proceeds + Other Foreclosure Proceeds

1.6.1 Data volume

The data analyzed in this study represents more than $2 trillion of conforming mortgages. The data made available by Fannie Mae and Freddie Mac captures a large share of their respective portfolios, but not the entirety. Figures 1.4 – 1.6 summarize the volume of loans in the data as well as defaults and default rate.

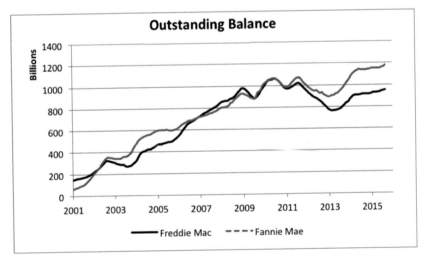

Figure 1.4. Outstanding balances for the data in the study from Fannie Mae and Freddie Mac.

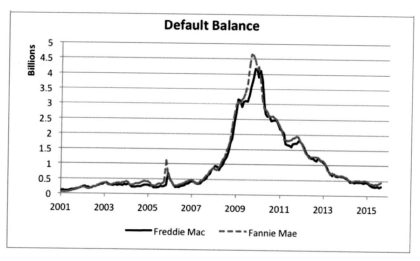

Figure 1.5. Default balances for the data in the study from Fannie Mae and Freddie Mac.

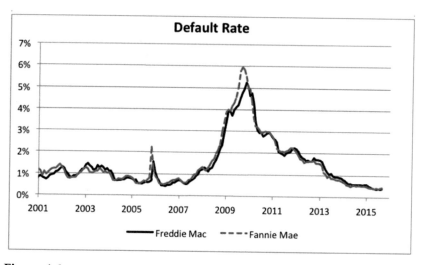

Figure 1.6. Annualized default rate for the data in the study from Fannie Mae and Freddie Mac.

1.6.2 Segmentation

All models were segmented by risk grade: Subprime is less than 660 FICO, Prime is 660 to 780, and Superprime is 780 and above. Figures 1.7 & 1.8 show the data by these segments.

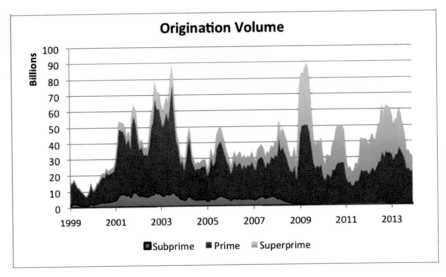

Figure 1.7. Booked accounts by risk grade.

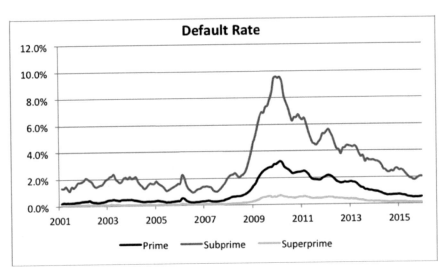

Figure 1.8. Annualized account default rate segmented by risk grade.

In addition to risk grade, all models were tested with either a single national model or segmented by US state. Figures 1.9 and 1.10 show show the data density by US state.

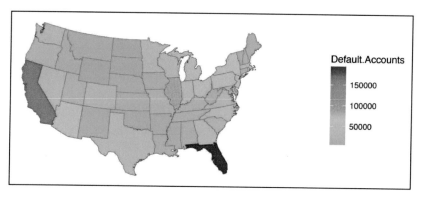

Figure 1.9. Default accounts by state for the full training data.

Figure 1.10. Average annualized account default rate by state for the training data.

1.7 Macroeconomic Data

As part of the government's implementation of the Dodd-Frank Stress Test Act (DFAST), the Federal Reserve Board regularly releases Base, Adverse, and Severe scenarios for a set of macroeconomic factors. Our expectation is that many lenders will choose to adopt the DFAST Base scenario for their CECL loss reserve estimation. Because these scenarios and factors have become industry standards, this study uses these factors for incorporating macroeconomic sensitivity.

Table 1.3 lists all of the available domestic macroeconomic factors available in the DFAST scenarios. The left column lists those factors most naturally related to mortgage performance and therefore considered in this study. The right column lists additional factors that are either re-

Mortgage-related Factors	Other Factors
Real gross domestic product (GDP) growth	Nominal GDP growth
Real disposable income growth	Nominal disposable income growth
Unemployment rate	CPI inflation rate
Mortgage rate	3-month Treasury rate
Dow Jones Total Stock Market Index	5-year Treasury yield
House Price Index	10-year Treasury yield
	BBB corporate yield
	Prime rate
	Commercial Real Estate Price Index (Level)
	Market Volatility Index (Level)
	Auto48 rate
	Credit Card rate
	Personal24 rate

Table 1.3. Domestic macroeconomic factors available in the DFAST scenarios.

dundant with the left column or less directly related to mortgage performance. The list of factors was restricted in this way to avoid overfitting when estimating the models.

Figures 1.11 – 1.14 show some of the key economic variables for modeling mortgage defaults including the 2016 DFAST scenarios.

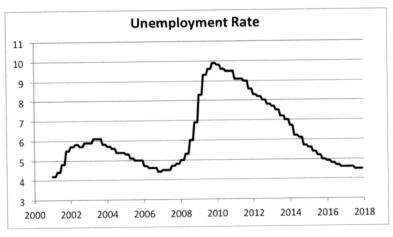

Figure 1.11. Historic unemployment rate (%) data with the DFAST base scenario appended in 2016.

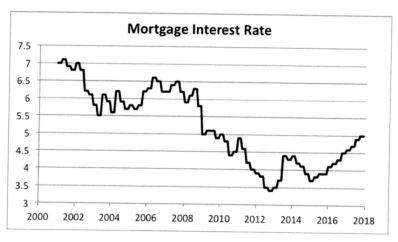

Figure 1.12. Historic mortgage interest rate (%) data with the DFAST base scenario beginning in 2016.

1.7.1 Macroeconomic data by US state

For modeling by geographic segmentation, state-level data for the DFAST factors was obtained from the Federal Reserve Economic Database (FRED). The DFAST national scenarios were apportioned to the states through a set of lead/lag and scaling models. Such models are not advertised as accurate state-level macroeconomic forecasting models, but they are sufficient to provide plausible state-level scenarios that are consistent with the DFAST national scenarios and past macroeconomic sensitivities.

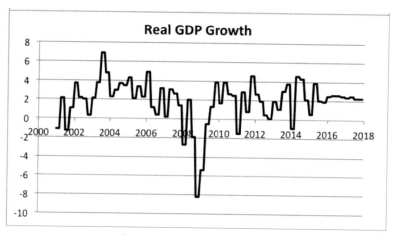

Figure 1.13. Historic real gross domestic product (RGDP) annualized growth rate (%) data with the DFAST base scenario beginning in 2016.

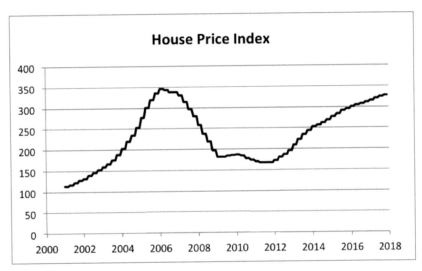

Figure 1.14. Historic house price index (HPI) data with the DFAST base scenario beginning in 2016.

1.7.2 Long-range scenarios

To extend beyond the foreseeable future, mean-reverting scenarios were created. The creation of mean-reverting scenarios is a straightforward procedure using either an Ornstein-Uhlenbeck process or a second order O-U process. Chapter 10 provides the technical details.

Usually, mean-reverting scenarios are created for individual macroeconomic factors based upon their historic performance. This process should be applied after the macroeconomic factor has been transformed to a stationary form. For example, mean-reversion is only sensible for HPI after applying a transformation like log-ratio (a symmetric rate of change transformation). These transformations usually include parameters, such as the time span over which the change is computed. Therefore, it is most natural to compute the mean-reverting scenario on the transformed macroeconomic factor after it has been optimized for forecasting.

However, from a model comparison perspective, creating standardized mean-reversion was one of the biggest challenges. Each model will have at least slightly different optimized transformations of the macroeconomic factors or may rely upon different factors entirely. This is no problem for creating forecasts with a single model, but trying to find differences between models may be lost in differences between the mean-reverting scenarios generated.

Therefore, a step was taken that is necessary only for the current study. Each model was created first to optimize all input factors, including macroeconomic factors. Then an index was created that collects all of the macroeconomic sensitivity of that model. For that index, which should be stationary by definition, a mean-reverting scenario was created. For example, in a roll rate model, the net roll from one month delinquent to two months delinquent is called Roll 2. That variable was modeled with macroeconomic factors, transformed and optimized for predictive accuracy. Those macroeconomic factors for Roll 2 were collected into an index and a mean reverting scenario created for the period beyond 24 months in the future. The same process was followed for each variable in each model.

2

Results Summary

The models were assessed via several criteria. The study's goal was not just to identify the most accurate model, because other considerations may be as much or more important than accuracy. Rather, institutions need a diverse set of criteria from which to perform their own cost-benefit analysis to choose a appropriate methodologies.

Therefore, this chapter summarizes the performance of the models along various dimensions: accuracy, complexity, level of lifetime forecast, and others. In addition, the effects of vintage analysis and discounting were measured. The magnitude of the transition from old to new rules was quantified along with how that transition changes through the economic cycle.

2.1 Model Accuracy

Several methods were used to assess model accuracy. No single perspective captures everything. Mostly notably, CECL is about creating a lifetime loss forecast, but even with this dataset, not enough data is available for a lifetime test.

2.1.1 In-sample accuracy with actual economic conditions

The first question for any model is how accurately it predicts. Table 2.1 shows the cumulative error over a three-year, in-sample forecast starting at three different points in the history. The starting points were selected to be just before the onset of the recession, at the peak of the recession, and during the recovery.

The moving average model, which computes the average balance default and pay-down rates of the previous twelve months, is shown only

Model	Jan 2007 – Dec 2014	Jul 2010 – Jun 2013	Jan 2012 – Dec 2009	Avg Absolute Error
Historic Average	−69.1%	54.1%	65.7%	63.0%
Time Series	11.2%	−28.7%	−12.5%	17.4%
Roll Rate	27.0%	−25.0%	−11.7%	21.2%
Vintage	3.6%	3.3%	1.9%	2.9%
State Transition	7.8%	11.1%	−1.3%	6.7%
Discrete Time Survival	−0.5%	4.5%	3.5%	2.8%

Table 2.1. The cumulative percentage error is shown over a three-year forecast period using the actual economic history. Results are for the nationwide models.

for comparison to common practice before CECL. As a model, moving averages are always out-of-phase with the economic cycle – the reason CECL was created.

Time series and roll rate models perform reasonably well, because they can capture the economic cycle, but not the credit cycle. Roll rate models can be expected to perform reasonably well for the first six to twelve months (better than a time series model) but that advantage disappears for long-lived forecasts such as are needed for 30-year mortgage. Such models may be usable depending upon the model acceptance criteria and the available data.

Vintage models incorporate variation in credit cycles and economic cycles, so their improved accuracy over roll rate and time series models for long-term forecasting is not a surprise. Loan-level models (State Transition and Discrete Time Survival) are more actionable than the preceding aggregate models, but not more accurate than vintage models when viewed in aggregate for the portfolio.

Model	Jan 2007 – Dec2009	Jul 2010 – Jun 2013	Jan 2012 – Dec 2014	Avg Absolute Error
Historic Average	−70.4%	54.3%	62.7%	62.4%
Time Series	19.4%	−26.1%	−12.9%	19.4%
Roll Rate	25.8%	−16.7%	−4.5%	15.7%
Vintage	−2.4%	1.2%	1.5%	1.3%
State Transition	−6.2%	12.5%	0%	6.3%
Discrete Time Survival	−3.8%	4.2%	2.9%	3.6%

Table 2.2. The cumulative percentage error is shown over a three-year forecast period using actual economic history. Results are for the US state-level models.

Table 2.2 conducts the same in-sample test for the state-level models. Segmenting by geography (US states) significantly increases the effort, but not the accuracy of the models. Of course, a state-level model will be more accurate than a national model when viewing only one state, but state-level analysis does not improve the result in aggregate. State-level analysis will be more actionable than a single national model, especially for lenders with a limited geographic footprint.

Few standards exist in model validation. No fixed threshold exists for how accurate is accurate enough. We can assume that the moving average model is not sufficient, but the other models require further review.

At the other extreme, the author has seen validation teams that require any accepted model to be within 2% error for a test such as this, or some similar criterion. From experience, we know such thresholds are rarely obtainable. Most often, modeling teams reach these objectives only through extensive over-fitting, inclusion of error correcting terms, or other tricks that do not capture the true out-of-sample performance of the model. With the models built here, no such tricks were incorporated. Each model was refined according to the usual practices of passing p-value thresholds on factors, multicolinearity tests, and so forth. The model structures were adjusted to provide a fair representation of the technique, but no hand-tuning was performed or other attempts made purely to enhance in-sample accuracy. Given this process, we consider the accuracies measured here to be representative of what lenders should expect when modeling their own data.

2.1.2 In-sample accuracy with economic scenarios

The preceding results used actual economic conditions for the in-sample testing. Practitioners will naturally be curious about how much change would occur if economic scenarios at the time of the forecast were used instead of actuals. In other words, what if we didn't know the future.

To answer this, historic scenarios were obtained from Consensus Economics. They regularly poll more than 25 economic forecast providers to create a consensus view for the subsequent two years. Using those consensus scenarios instead of the true economic values, Table 2.3 shows the change in the forecast for the first two years for each of the test periods.

The time series model showed the most sensitivity to the economic scenario, because it explains everything with economics. The other models are more consistent in having a roughly 15% variation during the first 24 months. As expected, the models all under-predicted losses dur-

Model	Jan 2007 – Dec 2008	Jul 2010 – Jun 2012	Jan 2012 – Dec 2013	Avg Absolute Error
Time Series	−18.3%	14.7%	60.6%	31.2%
Roll Rate	−20.8%	−0.3%	26.8%	16.0%
Vintage	−15.4%	5.2%	26.6%	15.7%
State Transition	−20.8%	−7.1%	0.4%	9.4%
Survival	−33.4%	−13.3%	3.7%	16.8%

Table 2.3. The change in the two-year forecast when switching from the historic macroeconomic data to the consensus macroeconomic scenario at the start of the forecast.

ing the 2009 recession, as the consensus economic projections under-predicted the severity of the recession. Well into the recovery, most models over-predict losses because of the over-prediction of economic weakness by economists.

In general, these results can be seen as a partial reversion from an accurate model under real economic conditions toward the historic average results that do not use economic scenarios. However, the modeled results with scenarios from economists are still significantly more accurate than not using models as in the historic average approach.

2.1.3 Accuracy by portfolio size

The state-level models provide an easy opportunity to test the scaling properties of the models to smaller datasets. Each point along the lines in Figures 2.1 – 2.3 represents the accuracy of the model for one state. The x-axis is the number of defaults in the training data. The y-axis is the error on a log scale, so that a random model would be at 10^0 and a model with 10% cumulative error over the three year forecast would be at 10^{-1}. The three graphs correspond to the three risk grade segments.

For the subprime and prime segments, above a number of defaults equal to $10^{3.5} \approx 3,000$, all models flatten out in accuracy. They have enough defaults to model and reach maximum accuracy. Of the three risk grades, the superprime segment goes to the most extreme limited data range and is worth further scrutiny.

Several patterns are apparent in the error scaling with volume. The time series model is relatively insensitive to the volume of training data, appearing as flat lines for the subprime, prime, and superprime segments. However, even adjusting for the volume of the training data, the subprime segment is easier to model with macroeconomic data than the prime segment, which in turn models better than the superprime segment.

The other models are more dynamic with the amount of training data, trending to higher error for small datasets but hitting an accuracy floor for larger datasets. Although all models show a similar pattern, the roll rate model consistently has the highest error. Although roll rates are assumed to be accurate over the first six months, those benefits do not persist through a three-year test such as this. The vintage and survival models perform well across the test ranges except for the most extreme small data regime. The state-transition model is consistently better than

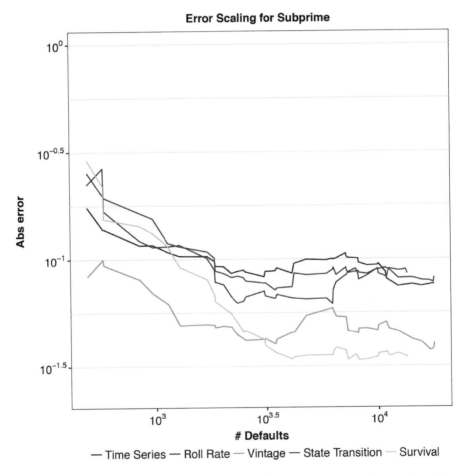

Figure 2.1. A comparison of model in-sample accuracy versus the number of charge-off accounts in the training set for the subprime risk segment.

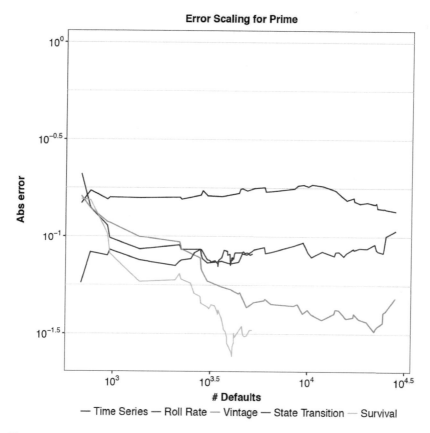

Figure 2.2. A comparison of model in-sample accuracy versus the number of charge-off accounts in the training set for the prime risk segment.

the roll rate model but generally weaker than the vintage and survival models.

2.1.4 Accuracy by forecast horizon

The previous tests were cumulative across a three-year horizon. Instead the results can be viewed as a function of forecast horizon. Figure 2.4 shows model accuracy averaged across all 52 states and territories, 3 risk grades, and 3 test periods. These results both confirm some conventional wisdom and show some surprises.

For the first three months of the forecast, the roll rate and state transition models are the clear winners. Since the target variable is default balance, current delinquency is the most important predictor of default for the first few months. By contrast, vintage and survival models are

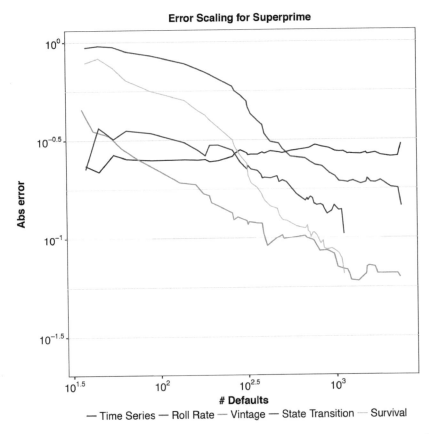

Figure 2.3. A comparison of model in-sample accuracy versus the number of charge-off accounts in the training set for the superprime risk segment.

looking across the full history, not just the most recent month, so they are prone to small discontinuities at the start of the forecast. Similarly, time series models are fit across the whole history prone to even larger discontinuities.

More surprising is how the models perform further into the forecast. At month four, all except the time series model have equal accuracy. By month six of the forecast, the model types have clearly diverged. The roll rate, state transition, and time series models deteriorate rapidly with forecast horizon, but the vintage and survival models are remarkably stable into to more distant future. The performance of the vintage and survival models is clearly due to the incorporation of a lifecycle, aka survival or hazard function. Beyond the first few months, this is the dominant predictor of default, scaled by credit risk.

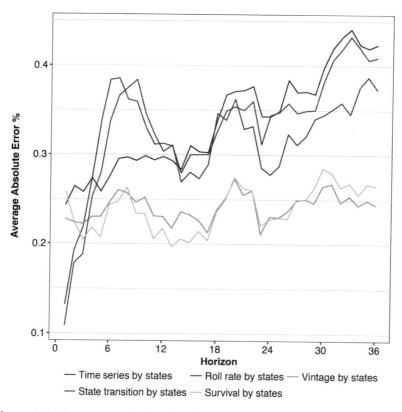

Figure 2.4. The average absolute forecast error is shown versus forecast horizon for each model, averaged across the 52 states and territories, three risk grades, and three test periods.

2.1.5 Backtesting

Out-of-sample testing, aka backtesting, is a required part of any model validation, but unfortunately it is often underwhelming in the outcome. Ideally one would like to have an out-of-sample recession to test against. Although two recessions are present in the data, the 2001 recession is not well enough represented in the data to create robust models for testing against the 2009 recession. Conversely, some model types would allow a model to be built on data from the 2009 recession and tested on the 2001 recession, but is not appropriate for others.

In most model validation efforts, the fallback position is to recreate the models holding out the last 12 months and test the forecast against those. Unfortunately, in a dataset such as this, the last 12 months have been mostly flat, and the winning approach might be nothing more than a moving average or ARMA model, because they minimize discontinuity to the start of the forecast, but have no predictive power through a recession.

Model	Segment			Total
	Prime	Subprime	Superprime	
Time Series	−13%	−7%	−16%	−12%
Roll Rate	25%	1%	7%	18%
Vintage	18%	23%	6%	18%
State Transition	52%	31%	74%	49%
Survival	13%	10%	2%	11%

Table 2.4. Cumulative 12-month out-of-sample accuracy for predicting default balance.

To comply with industry norms, Table 2.4 provides a 12-month out-of-sample backtest for default balance where only actual economic conditions are included through the forecast period. Since none of these models included moving average error terms, this just measures how far the economic model based only upon DFAST variables has drifted from performance actuals in the recent months. Therefore, it is a test only of whether the DFAST economic factors are rich enough to capture the most recent trends. Based upon results across the retail lending industry, it appears that the DFAST variables are, in fact, not sufficiently complete. Most notably they lack a measure of consumer debt burden, which has been trending higher and appears to correlate to recent forecast errors.

2.2 Foreseeable Period

The foreseeable period is not specified in the CECL guidelines or in IFRS 9. We used 24 months as the foreseeable period everywhere except this section just because it seems to be a common value for IFRS 9. The concept of a foreseeable period makes sense relative to macroeconomic scenarios, although it seems that some institutions also take it to be what is foreseeable by the models. As seen in the accuracy test by forecast horizon, Section 2.1.4, that approach is very model-dependent.

The results in Tables 2.5 – 2.7 show what lifetime loss forecasts would have been obtained using different values for the foreseeable period. For each test, actual historical macroeconomic data was used, so this does not test the ability of economists to choose an accurate scenario. In each case, the macroeconomic scenarios are reverted to the long-run average at the end of the test period.

Model	Test	Foreseeable	Lifetime Loss Rate	Change
Time Series	Jan-07	12	0.99%	
Time Series	Jan-07	24	1.14%	0.15%
Time Series	Jan-07	36	1.67%	0.53%
Time Series	Jul-10	12	1.71%	
Time Series	Jul-10	24	1.71%	0.00%
Time Series	Jul-10	36	1.71%	0.00%
Time Series	Jan-12	12	0.95%	
Time Series	Jan-12	24	1.02%	0.07%
Time Series	Jan-12	36	1.00%	−0.02%
Time Series	Jan-16	12	0.77%	
Time Series	Jan-16	24	0.78%	0.01%
Time Series	Jan-16	36	0.79%	0.02%

Table 2.5. Changes in the lifetime loss estimates by varying the foreseeable period for the Time Series model.

Model	Test	Foreseeable	Lifetime Loss Rate	Change
Roll Rates	Jan-07	12	1.52%	
Roll Rates	Jan-07	24	1.84%	0.32%
Roll Rates	Jan-07	36	2.35%	0.51%
Roll Rates	Jul-10	12	2.27%	
Roll Rates	Jul-10	24	2.00%	−0.26%
Roll Rates	Jul-10	36	1.91%	−0.09%
Roll Rates	Jan-12	12	1.28%	
Roll Rates	Jan-12	24	1.28%	0.01%
Roll Rates	Jan-12	36	1.20%	−0.08%
Roll Rates	Jan-16	12	1.15%	
Roll Rates	Jan-16	24	1.19%	0.04%
Roll Rates	Jan-16	36	1.23%	0.05%

Table 2.6. Changes in the lifetime loss estimates by varying the foreseeable period for the Roll Rate model.

The results are interesting in their irrelevance. Table 2.5 shows the test results for the time series model. Increasing the foreseeable period can increase or decrease the lifetime loss rate. The Change column shows how much the rates change relative to the 12-month result.

Model	Test	Foreseeable	Lifetime Loss Rate	Change
Vintage	Jan-07	12	1.34%	
Vintage	Jan-07	24	1.52%	0.18%
Vintage	Jan-07	36	1.91%	0.39%
Vintage	Jul-10	12	2.33%	
Vintage	Jul-10	24	2.38%	0.05%
Vintage	Jul-10	36	2.35%	−0.03%
Vintage	Jan-12	12	1.65%	
Vintage	Jan-12	24	1.62%	−0.03%
Vintage	Jan-12	36	1.61%	−0.01%
Vintage	Jan-16	12	0.89%	
Vintage	Jan-16	24	0.90%	0.00%
Vintage	Jan-16	36	0.91%	0.02%

Table 2.7. Changes in the lifetime loss estimates by varying the foreseeable period for the Vintage model.

Table 2.8 shows the variability by model type and foreseeable period, measured as the maximum loss rate minus the minimum rate across the test periods. It shows that the variability of the result is almost identical for 12, 24, and 36 month foreseeable periods. In other words, none of these is more or less volatile. This could be a surprising result. The roll rate result shows more variability, but not in a systematic way. The vintage model results show the same lack of variability as the time series model.

Model	Foreseeable period		
	12	24	36
Time Series	0.94%	0.94%	0.92%
Roll Rates	1.12%	0.82%	1.15%
Vintage	1.44%	1.49%	1.44%

Table 2.8. Forecast variability through the economic cycle with different foreseeable periods used in the calculation

The conclusion seems to be that one variability estimate for the roll rate model was an outlier. Overall, the lifetime loss estimates, when averaged through the economic cycle, do not really depend upon the foreseeable period because the mean-reversion always acts to offset extreme macroeconomic scenarios.

These results argue that one cannot choose the foreseeable period to raise, lower, or reduce the volatility of the CECL estimates. From the accuracy versus horizon tests, we should choose the model that is accurate through the foreseeable period, not the other way around. Furthermore, the reliability of management plans does not factor into the choice of the foreseeable period, because only the existing portfolio is being modeled. No future underwriting decisions matter.

That leaves the final criterion for selecting the period as the reliability of macroeconomic scenarios. As seen in the test of using actual macroeconomic scenarios, economists through the last cycle under-predicted the severity of the recession and the magnitude of the recovery. A visual inspection of the scenarios suggests that already in the second year the scenarios begin to look like a reversion to average performance. Relying on economic scenarios beyond 24 months is probably not substantially different from using mean-reversion during that period.

2.3 Model Complexity

Accuracy often comes at a price in complexity. To measure model complexity, Table 2.9 simply sums the total number of coefficients required for each model. This does not capture the complexity in algorithms or software required, but we have few meaningful metrics for that.

Model	Total # of coefficients	
	National	State-level
Time Series	33	2,159
Roll Rate	129	6,265
Vintage	69	2,628
State Transition	2,097	75,455
Discrete Time Survival	240	11,551

Table 2.9. The total number of estimated coefficients is shown for each national and state-level model.

The vintage model has fewer coefficients than might be expected, because the nonparametric lifecycles are simple enough to replace with a small number of spline coefficients and the environment function was replaced with a simple macroeconomic model.

The state transition model has the largest number of coefficients, because of all the separate transitions being modeled. Various simplifications on state transition modeling exist, all designed to lower the number of estimated coefficients required, but generally at a cost of some in-sample accuracy.

The state-level models just scale up the number of coefficients for the 50 independent states being modeled. This could be simplified greatly by including panel model aspects in the design. Having fully independent models is used as an upper bound on the complexity and accuracy for all these approaches.

2.4 Computation Time

The models require different amounts of computation time. Times given below in Table 2.10 are to run one forecast on one 2.5 GHz processor of a server with 240 GB of RAM. Significant effort was made to optimize the code for the State Transition and Discrete Time Survival models.

Model	Computation time (min)	
	National	State-level
Time Series	3	9
Roll Rate	3	10
Vintage	10	35
State Transition	1,110	1,680
Discrete Time Survival	270	390

Table 2.10. The time needed to run a single forecast for each model is shown.

Overall, the computation time scales with the level of aggregation. Time series to roll rate to vintage is a smooth increase in computation time. Discrete time survival and state transition models are applied at the loan-level, with many more variables being estimated for state transition, so the table affords no real surprises.

2.5 Model Completeness

For time series models, to test for model completeness, practitioners typically apply the Durbin–Watson Gujarati (Durbin and Watson 1950; 1951, Gujarati and Porter 2009) or Ljung–Box (Ljung and Box 1978) tests. These tests measure the significance of autocorrelation in the model residuals. Although useful in one-dimension, they do not address the current context where residuals can be viewed across vintages as well as through time. In the context of CECL, the possibility of residual correlated structure across vintages takes on added meaning.

When model residuals are viewed by vintage and time or equivalently age and time, correlation can be measured via a spatial correlation test (Breeden 2010). The residuals of any model may be computed in these two dimensions to test for completeness in forecasting vintages. One such method that preserves the standard range and interpretation for correlation values is Moran's I(d) (Moran 1950).

$$I(d) = \frac{\sum_{a \text{ or } v} \sum_{t} (\epsilon_j - \bar{\epsilon})(\epsilon_j - \bar{\epsilon})}{\sum_j (\epsilon_j - \bar{\epsilon})^2} \qquad (2.1)$$

In this formula, ϵ_j is the residual at a location in age and time or vintage and time, and the summations are across those dimensions for which the distance is within a given band. The distance between two points in age and time is defined by the following formula.

$$d = \sqrt{\delta t^2 + \delta a^2 - \delta t \delta a} \qquad (2.2)$$

Null hypotheses can be created by randomizing and reanalyzing the residuals, so as to allow for non-normal distributions of the residuals.

Figure 2.5 shows the correlation of the residuals for the models developed in the study. The dotted black line shows the 5% and 95% null hypothesis values for 100 reshufflings. The errors, ϵ_j, were the combined average forecast error for each of the three test periods and all three segments.

Immediately we see that none of the models are perfect. They all have residual spatial correlation across the age and time dimensions. Each model will have a different reason for such errors, but the overall levels fit an expected pattern.

The time series model does not consider vintages or delinquency and has the highest residual correlation of all the models. The roll rate model improves upon this, but still with significant error. The improvements continue through the state transition model and vintage model until the discrete time survival model is reached as the one with the lowest residual correlation. None of the models include moving average terms on the fit to macroeconomic factors, so correlated errors are expected due to industry-wide changes in unobserved factors. This was done intentionally so as to demonstrate what was possible with the data available. Overall, these results are consistent with the summary forecast accuracies in Section 2.1.

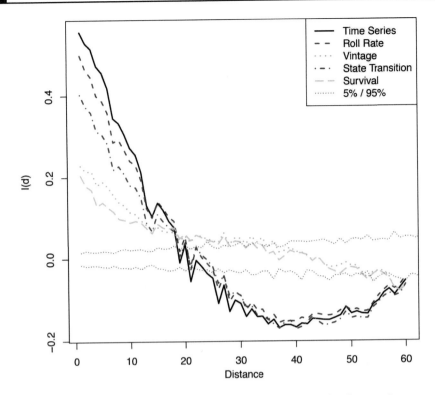

Figure 2.5. Spatial correlation of residuals in age and time. The distance is measured in months. The results for each model are compared to the null hypothesis in the dotted line.

2.6 Lifetime Loss Estimate

Even comparably accurate models on the three-year test may produce different lifetime loss estimates because of their long range extrapolation properties. This is particularly true for a product like 30-year mortgage. Although the first 15 years can be estimated from the data, the last 15 years are determined entirely by the intrinsic extrapolation properties of the model.

The preceding tests were conducted with two-year actual macroeconomic values, reverting onto long-run average levels to predict the pool from the forecast start date through the end of term or zero balance. All estimates assume 70% recovery rates. No discounting has been applied. Table 2.11 shows these lifetime loss forecasts for the national models.

Table 2.12 shows the same results for the state-level models. The aggregate results are not noticeably different between the national and state-level models when totaled.

Model, National	Jan-07	Jul-10	Jan-12	Jan-16
Historic Average	0.82%	7.14%	2.77%	1.03%
Time Series	1.14%	1.71%	1.02%	0.78%
Roll Rate	1.84%	2.00%	1.28%	1.19%
Vintage	1.52%	2.38%	1.62%	0.90%
State Transition	1.91%	2.63%	2.18%	1.64%
Discrete Time Survival	1.47%	2.34%	1.59%	0.63%
Actual	2.02%	> 1.8%		

Table 2.11. The CECL lifetime loss estimates from the national models are shown starting from different historic points. For historic estimates, real economic data was used for the first two years with mean reversion thereafter. For the January 2016 estimate, the FRB baseline scenario was used for the first two years. Actual values are known approximately only for the first two test periods.

Model, State-level	Jan-07	Jul-10	Jan-12	Jan-16
Historic Average	0.73%	6.66%	2.81%	1.09%
Time Series	1.75%	1.90%	1.23%	1.03%
Roll Rate	2.06%	2.15%	1.39%	1.10%
Vintage	1.50%	2.38%	1.64%	0.91%
State Transition	1.51%	2.26%	1.77%	1.08%
Discrete Time Survival	1.38%	2.31%	1.59%	0.68%
Actual	2.02%	> 1.8%		

Table 2.12. The CECL lifetime loss estimates from the state-level models are shown starting from different historic points. For historic estimates, real economic data was used for the first two years with mean reversion thereafter. For the January 2016 estimate, the FRB baseline scenario was used for the first two years. Actual values are known approximately only for the first two test periods.

2.7 Effect of Discounted Cash Flows

The options given for computing loss reserves under CECL include discounted cash flows. Discounting as an economics concept seems useful when considering a lifetime loss calculation. Distant future losses or payments should be less important than near-term losses or payments considering the time value of money.

As described in Section 1.4.3, discounting was considered in two ways:

1. Directly discounting the loss estimates. The monthly expected loss forecasts could be discounted and then summed to a total discounted loss.

2. Discounting the payment stream, aka discounted cash flows. The existing forecasts of attrition and charge-off are used to adjust the likelihood of receiving scheduled payments. These adjusted payment forecasts are then discounted, summed, and compared to the outstanding balance. This is the approach accountants think of when discussing Discounted Cash Flows (DCF).

Recoveries in this study are assumed to be 70% of the balance charged-off six months prior. This is a rough approximation, but recovery modeling is not a target of the current study.

Calculation	Jan-07	Jul-10	Jan-12	Jan-16
Simple Cumulative Loss	5.06%	7.93%	5.39%	2.98%
Discounted Losses	3.60%	6.37%	4.26%	2.23%
Ratio to Simple Cumulative	0.71	0.8	0.79	0.75
Discounted Cash Flow	1.28%	1.96%	1.40%	1.26%
Ratio to Simple Cumulative	0.25	0.25	0.26	0.42

Table 2.13. For the vintage model, a comparison is shown for the simple cumulative loss forecast, discounted losses, and discounted cash flow. The columns indicate different starting points for the lifetime loss forecast.

The results in Table 2.13 show that directly discounting the loss stream would lower the lifetime loss reserve by 20 to 30% depending upon the starting point for the calculation. The discounted cash flow approach results in significantly lower loss reserves, 60 to 75% below the original loss estimate.

From a theoretical perspective, we cannot say which approach is more appropriate. Discounting cash flows is more common for securitized loans, because a net present value calculation is needed for loan pricing. In the present context that starting point may not be necessary. Regardless of which approach is used, lenders will likely prefer the lower numbers from discounting, and CECL provides justification.

The DCF calculations here do not include other income sources such as late fees. For mortgage lending, those are generally viewed as minor in comparison to interest income. However for line of credit products such as credit cards, penalty fees are a substantial portion of the cash flows. A DCF approach to line of credit products would probably need to include modeling of the range of non-interest fees.

2.8 CECL versus "old rules"

One of the primary considerations for CECL adoption is the magnitude of the change from the old ALLL calculations under FAS 5 (ASC 450-20) to the new rules under CECL. Historically most lenders below roughly $10 billion in assets have used simple historic averages of their loss rates (look-back models) to set their baseline ALLL numbers before adding manual adjustments. Therefore, the comparison in Table 2.14 assumes that an average loss rate for the previous 12 months was used with a 24 month loss emergence period to set loss reserves under FAS 5. The lifetime loss numbers from the vintage model are used as the CECL benchmark.

	Segment	Jan-07	Jul-10	Jan-12	Jan-16	TTC Avg
Lifetime Loss						
	Subprime	512%	73%	17%	123%	181%
	Prime	1219%	95%	9%	217%	385%
	Superprime	1933%	160%	5%	210%	577%
	Total	896%	91%	11%	196%	299%
DCF						
	Subprime	57%	−57%	−60%	−59%	−30%
	Prime	240%	−52%	−64%	370%	123%
	Superprime	236%	−42%	−74%	65%	46%
	Total	153%	−53%	−63%	68%	26%

Table 2.14. The comparison is shown for a simple moving average approach under FAS 5 with a 24 month loss emergence period and a lifetime loss calculation under CECL using the vintage model with direct loss forecasts and discounted cash flows. The final column shows the Through-the-cycle (TTC) average.

With direct loss forecasting, the increases are dramatic, because lifetime losses for 30-year mortgage are much higher than 24-month losses. The increases are highest going into a recession, because the old models reserve at pre-recession levels. Levels are high in better-than-average economic environments because of reverting to through-the-cycle levels after two years. Loss reserves are roughly equal during improving economic conditions, because the old models over-reserve during this time.

With the discounted cash flow approach, the same patterns exist through the economic cycle, but with significantly lower estimates. Therefore, the DCF approach has an overall average increase of 26% whereas the average increase with direct aggregation of lifetime loss forecasts is 299%. DCF for CECL would even have lower loss reserves for subprime through the recession as compared to FAS 5.

2.9 Implications for IFRS 9

IFRS 9 (IASB 2014) is the new international standard for setting loan loss reserves. At its heart, IFRS 9 is stress testing, if the right models are used. IFRS 9 has three stages for loss estimation: Stage 1 for accounts performing as expected, Stage 2 for accounts exhibiting increased risk, and Stage 3 for impaired accounts.

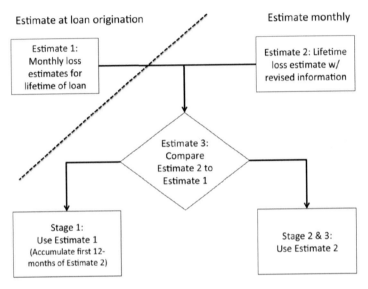

Figure 2.6. Diagram showing the various estimations needed when implementing IFRS 9. The dashed line separates one-time estimation from recurring estimates.

To satisfy IFRS 9, four estimates are required, as explained here and illustrated in Figure 2.6.

Estimate 1: Monthly loss estimates at origination through the life of the loan to determine the initial risk of the accounts. Since older accounts did not receive such estimates at origination, they must be retroactively assessed.

Estimate 2: A revised lifetime loss estimate at any subsequent age using macroeconomic conditions at that time with a mean-reverting algorithm to create the macroeconomic scenarios beyond the foreseeable future.

Estimate 3: If Estimate 2 is significantly higher than the Estimate 1 for the same time span (remaining life of the loan) and has a significant estimated loss, then the account is promoted to Stage 2. All Stage 2 and 3 accounts are reserved with this lifetime loss estimate.

Estimate 4: A 12-month ECL estimate for Stage 1 accounts.

All of the above estimations can be created from a single model if well chosen. The model should create monthly, loan-level estimates of expected loss from which all of the above requirements can be satisfied. The lifetime loss estimate "at origination" (Estimate 1) will mean applying the model to all accounts using macroeconomic scenarios appropriate as of their origination dates. Estimate 2 will use the same lifetime loss estimate but with macroeconomic scenarios appropriate for the start of the forecast. For Estimate 3, lenders often use a rule of thumb that a threshold for deterioration in loss estimation should be chosen such that on average through the economic cycle roughly 80% of accounts are Stage 1, and 20% of accounts should be classified as Stage 2. For Stage 2 and Stage 3 accounts, the lifetime loss estimate is used for loss reserves. Estimate 4 is obtained by using the same models applied to the Stage 1 accounts with only a 12-month horizon to compute loss reserves.

Given the need to compare initial loss estimates to current loss estimates, IFRS 9 implementations focus on vintage and survival models. The Stage 2 selection mechanism in Estimate 3 naturally seems to imply a loan-level model, but the selection can also be made in aggregate on entire vintages.

Faced with the complexities of IFRS 9 and 10,000+ US financial institutions, FASB opted for the simpler approach in CECL. Except for the nuances around lines-of-credit, CECL is IFRS 9 Stage 2. Therefore, the current study would appear to be very relevant to the creation of IFRS 9 models. Given the relatively good performance of vintage and survival models, this study would appear to confirm the predominant choices being made for IFRS 9 implementations.

2.10 Implications for other products

Thirty-year mortgages are probably the worst case for the new CECL rules. Even though the average life of such loans is about six years, this is substantially longer than most other loan types. Therefore, other loan types will not be equally impacted, but some extrapolations can be made.

2.10.1 Other term loans

The increase in loss reserves under CECL could be obtained from a back-of-the-envelop calculation. Comparing a six-year average life to a two-year loss emergence period under FAS 5 immediately yields a 3× increase in loss reserves. The rest is estimation details. For auto loans, preliminary analysis of customer data has shown that an average lifetime of 2.5 years compared to a loss emergence period of 12 months gives a 2.5× increase in loss reserves. For installment products, a rough estimate of the CECL impacts is as simple as comparing average lifetime to previously used loss emergence period.

From a modeling perspective, the accuracy versus forecast horizon in Table 2.4 provides interesting insights. For long-lived assets, vintage and survival models are the clear winners. The use of a lifecycle provides the accuracy needed to forecast beyond the four month cross-over point. For short-lived assets, such as pay-day loans, tax refund loans, and any term loan with a duration of six months or less, a roll rate or state transition model is best.

2.10.2 Lines of credit

Although CECL appears to be very like IFRS 9 Stage 2 calculations, they diverge in one very important aspect. CECL will handle lines-of-credit quite differently, because of the treatment of future purchases. Unlike IFRS 9, CECL applies only to the current loan balance and any undrawn line that cannot be canceled at will by the lender. For a credit card, home equity line, or business line of credit where the undrawn line can be frozen essentially instantly, CECL loss estimation only needs to consider the current balance. This has many dramatic consequences.

The CECL guidelines state that loss reserves should only cover the non-cancellable period. Credit cards for example are typically cancellable at any time, so the loss reserves would apply only to the current balance. Thus, the loss estimate for a $0 balance credit card is $0. New or unused cards are risk-free under CECL.

The challenging question is, for those lines with a balance, if the current balance were treated as a loan, what would the pay-down period be? Should all future payments be considered as payments against the current balance, or should only the portion exceeding future purchases be considered?

Initial comments from FASB appear to allow a range of approaches. Both of the following appear to be allowed:

- Future payments apply to the current balance only, or first-in-first-out (FIFO)

- Future payments in excess of future purchases or the required minimum payments apply to the current balance, or last-in-first-out (LIFO)

Of these options, the first will clearly produce the lowest loss reserves. In fact, when no future purchases are considered, the effective life of loan for credit card transactors (those who historically have paid off their balances every month) will be a single month. For revolvers (those who carry a monthly balance) the average life of loan can be several years. Therefore, the net life of loan for a credit card portfolio is sensitive to the transactor-revolver ratio.

One can take a deeper philosophical view of this process. Transactors almost never default, because they are financially able to pay the full balance each month. Defaults almost always come from a sequence of transactor to partial revolver to minimum payer and eventually to charge-off when minimum payments are no longer possible. This sequence is driven by rising outstanding balance. The balance upon which the consumer is making minimum payments is invariably higher than the balance during the time when they were a transactor.

Under CECL, the guidelines could be read to mean either that no new purchases are considered or that no line utilization growth is considered. For transactors, no new purchases mean that default is almost impossible. However, if no higher line utilization is considered, then the migration to revolver is also exceedingly rare. Although in theory we could create a model that captured the state transitions of transactor -> revolver -> min-payer -> default, if the data was filtered to capture only those accounts making this transition without increased line utilization, almost no defaults would be observed from transactor.

Therefore, regardless of the interpretation followed, transactors, and equivalently, recent accounts who have not grown balances, will have essentially zero loss reserves. Reserves will be generated predominantly from the min-payers and partial revolvers.

From a modeling perspective, transactors follow a short-term process, so they would seem to be a natural fit for a roll rate model. However, since transactors by definition are not delinquent, a roll rate model would have nothing to roll. Instead, one could estimate a simple PD rate filtering for current transactor who default in the future without growing their balances – practically 0%. Revolvers and min-payers in particular require the real modeling effort. Those losses will come over the long term, starting from when the account becomes a revolver.

Normally, vintage models would be recommended for long-range forecasting of line-of-credit products. They have an excellent track record in forecasting and stress testing, but they generally are not used in transactor / revolver models. The lifecycle for default probability is generally capturing the risk of transitioning from transactor to revolver, but if no forecast is required until a revolver state is reached, then the lifecycle may disappear. Therefore, the best approach to line-of-credit modeling warrants further research.

Another implication of the above interpretation is that lenders do not need to consider any future line increases. Even if current policy is to grant annual line increases of some average amount, CECL diverges from both CCAR and IFRS 9 in assuming no future increases.

Of course, these estimates are not appropriate from a portfolio management perspective. Actual 12-month losses may be significantly higher than CECL-estimated losses. In other words, CECL is not a prediction of lifetime losses for all active lines-of-credit. Rather, it is a specific loss reserve calculation capturing a portion of those future losses that are more tangibly foreseeable today. Lenders should not use CECL-estimated losses for pricing line-of-credit products.

2.10.3 Commercial lending

The majority of the analysis in this study is about retail loans and lines rather than commercial loans and lines. The primary reason for this dichotomy is the dominance of the lifecycle effect in retail lending. For every retail loan type, including small business loans, the age of the loan is a strong predictor of the risk of default. The lifecycles are different depending upon the details of the product, but tend to be very similar when compared across different lenders offering the same product.

The existence of these lifecycles is more difficult to explain. If one goes through a library of these, product by product, segment by segment, many of the features are not financially rational. Consumer behavior always includes aspects of personal utility. Just because my home is not worth what I paid for it, there is no certainty that I will default if I can still afford the mortgage. If I defaulted, where would I live? Why uproot my family just because someone tells me that I overpaid? In fact, my mortgage lender very helpfully sent me a letter with an estimate showing the my home value was underwater and therefore they were freezing my unused home equity line. It's almost as if they were daring me to make the financially optimal decision of defaulting.

Strategic default, where consumers default if the asset is not worth the purchase price, largely does not apply to homes, cars, or credit cards. Most of the examples of strategic default on mortgages in the last recession were either recent purchases where consumers had no established roots or investment properties that the buyer hoped to flip. For consumers, that perspective is the exception, not the rule.

Commercial lending is different. Decisions on loan repayment are made for much more financially rigorous reasons, usually by a financial professional. Of course, someone owning commercial property will likely continue to keep making payments so long as rent or other income received continues to generate a reasonable return. This is part of the rational financial calculation.

Perhaps because commercial lending is dominated by financial calculations rather than human lifestyle decisions, commercial loan products rarely exhibit a lifecycle. Losses do exhibit a dependence on the age of the loan, but only over long time scales and with nothing more than gentle trends. The dramatic structures of auto loans and credit cards are absent. Because of the slow and featureless lifecycles, simpler methods are effective. Grade migration and panel data methods tend to dominate.

The challenge for commercial lending is not the modeling but the lack of data. Many portfolios have experienced only single-digit or double-digit numbers of defaults through their history, meaning that only the simplest methods can be employed. For commercial real estate, some loan-level industry data exists, and for all products industry time series are available, but few lenders will be able to create purely in-house, owned-portfolio only models.

2.11 Model Risk Management for CECL

Model risk management became a hot topic in the banking industry after the spectacular failures of so many loss reserve models in the US Mortgage Crisis. It's not enough to build a model, you need to show that it is sound and effective, and you need to decide what the criteria are for sound and effective before beginning to build a model. With the dramatic changes planned for computing loan loss reserves under CECL, model risk management should again be top of mind.

One of the primary regulatory documents on model risk management is SR 11-7 (FRB 2011). This lays out the fundamentals for model risk management and modern governance. The following excerpt is relevant, because even before smaller organizations implement CECL, they must develop a model risk management plan. This study was part of such a plan, as is clear from the requirements below.

- **Evaluation of Conceptual Soundness.** This element involves assessing the quality of the model design and construction, as well as review of documentation and empirical evidence supporting the methods used and variables selected for the model. This step in validation should ensure that judgment exercised in model design and construction is well informed, carefully considered, and consistent with published research and with sound industry practice.

- **Ongoing Monitoring.** This step in validation is done to confirm that the model is appropriately implemented and is being used and performing as intended. It is essential to evaluate whether changes in products, exposures, activities, clients, or market conditions necessitate adjustment, redevelopment, or replacement of the model and to verify that any extension of the model beyond its original scope is valid. Benchmarking can be used in this step to compare a given model's inputs and outputs to estimates from alternatives.

- **Outcomes Analysis.** This step involves comparing model outputs to corresponding actual outcomes. Back-testing is one form of outcomes analysis that involves the comparison of actual outcomes with model forecasts during a sample time period not used in model development at a frequency that matches the model's forecast horizon or performance window.

The results of the three core elements of the validation process may reveal significant errors or inaccuracies in model development or outcomes that consistently fall outside the banking organization's predetermined thresholds of acceptability. In such cases, model adjustment, recalibration, or redevelopment is warranted. At times, banking organizations may have a limited ability to use key model validation tools for various reasons, such as lack of data or of price observability. In those cases, even more attention should be paid to the model's limitations when considering the appropriateness of model usage, and senior management should be fully informed of those limitations when using the models for decision-making.

Numerous books, articles, and presentations are available on model risk management (Bennett 2017, Scandizzo 2016). Past regulatory guidance has made clear that all models require effective model risk management practices covering development, validation, and governance (FDIC 2017, FRB 2011, OCC 2011). CECL will not be an exception:

> ...where models and model output have a material impact on business decisions, including decisions related to risk management and capital and liquidity planning, and where model failure would have a particularly harmful impact on a bank's financial condition, a bank's model risk management framework should be more extensive and rigorous.

The above quote from SR 11-7 leaves no doubt that model risk management will be important for CECL Of course, the guidelines also allow for scaling the intensity of the model risk management process to the importance of the models and size of the lender. Clearly, CECL models will be high importance overall, but not equally so for smaller portfolios. Likewise, smaller lenders will have lower overall requirements, but some level of model risk management will always be required.

Another valuable passage from SR 11-7 is:

> An integral part of model development is testing, in which the various components of a model and its overall functioning are evaluated to show the model is performing as intended; to demonstrate that it is accurate, robust, and stable; and to evaluate its limitations and assumptions.

To confirm that "the model is performing as intended", one must have an intent. As larger lenders have iterated through implementing model risk management, they have bootstrapped their way to guidelines and expectations on what constitutes an effective model. Now, the acceptance criteria already exist for any new model that will be developed. The lesson for those creating model risk management practices for CECL is simple. Before you build a model, decide how you will know if it is good.

With this as background, we often hear lenders about to implement CECL say, "Every conference that I go to says that I must implement all of the CECL models and choose which is best for my portfolio." Unfortunately, these are well-meaning platitudes for a conference presentation that are unhelpful in many ways.

First, there is no such thing as "all the CECL models". Yes, the CECL guidelines list examples of models, but SR 16-12 by the Federal Reserve, OCC, and NCUA clearly states, "Similar to the existing incurred losses model, the new accounting standard does not prescribe the use of specific estimation methods." The list of models given in the FASB document is stated in many places as an "example". Nevertheless, assuming that one wants to implement multiple models, the encouragement to "choose the best for my portfolio" leaves one wondering, "How will you choose?" The two most common answers are:

1. "The one I like best"

2. "The one that forecasts best"

The first answer clearly violates model risk management practice. Even worse is when lenders say, "I want multiple models so that I can choose which answer I like best each time." Epic fail. This is not how model risk management works.

For a model to be accepted, you must have clear criteria for selection. They can be a mix of quantitative and qualitative factors, but "We like the number" should not be on the list. As the current study proves, the answer can change dramatically by model type, but the reasons for choosing a model should be based on sound model risk management practices. Furthermore, once you have chosen a model, do not expect to be able to change models without sound reasons, i.e. a study was conducted that proved the alternate model was better for the following reasons.... Therefore, major lenders usually have a primary model, a challenger model where there are trying to resolve weaknesses in the primary model for the next release, and a benchmark model offering a sanity check on the results. Managing these three models is already a significant effort. Having more makes little sense.

The second criteria of "The one that forecasts best" sounds like a good idea, but there are several problems. CECL is a lifetime loss reserve calculation. The CECL number incorporates decisions, such as the distinction between foreseeable and unforeseeable, that have nothing to do with forecast accuracy. Also, as a lifetime loss forecast, we cannot expect to wait for the full life of a loan or have enough historic data to determine if the forecast was accurate. Many lenders are just now creating history for CECL modeling. Even if they have as much as five years of history, this would not capture a full economic cycle and would not allow for a full test of a five year auto loan, credit card, or longer term products. Conversely, a 12-month forecast accuracy test usually captures only the degree of discontinuity between the economic model and the most recent data. Clearly, for many lenders, even having enough data in-sample to estimate a model may be a stretch. How then should they "choose"?

Actually, this gets to the fundamental purpose of this study and others like it that are under way. Figures 2.1 – 2.3 showing how accuracy scales with the volume of charge-offs in the training data and Figure 2.4 showing how error grows with forecast horizon are solid, quantified information to allow lenders to choose a model type where their internal data may not allow a sound decision to be made. My advice to lenders, from a model risk management approach, is to use this study and those like it to filter out the approaches that will be hopeless on the available data, establish the criteria for which the best model will be chosen, and then dedicate the necessary resources to build a couple of appropriate model types—in that order.

2.12 Test Conclusions

Projecting losses via time series models of default and pay-down rates produced an average 3-year cumulative error rate of 17-19%. In itself, that will raise concerns with validators, but the accuracy is unchanging relative to the amount of training data, which can be useful for very small or noisy datasets. Vintage models were consistently high performers in terms of accuracy with 1% to 3% error rates. Discrete time survival models and state transition models both perform well (6.5% to 7.5%), but not better than vintage models, showing that loan-level modeling does not guarantee more accuracy. Vintage, state transition, and survival models all had similar scaling properties versus size of training data. Roll rate models were consistently the worst performers at 15% to 20% error rates. Moving averages of historic loss rates are unsuited to lifetime loss forecasting at 60+% error rates. Overall, roll rate and historic average models should not be used for long-lived products.

Creating separate models by US state did not provide greater accuracy when compared to a single national model of the same portfolio. Geographic segmentation provided advantages in business application but not model accuracy.

The guidelines state that vintage modeling is not a requirement. If we assume that "vintage model" refers to any approach that adjusts credit risk and prepayment risk based upon the age of the loan, then the results show significant increases in accuracy for techniques incorporating this (vintage models, state-transition models, and discrete time survival models) as compared to those that do not include it (time series and roll rates). The loan-level models (state transition and survival) were by far the most complex in terms of numbers of coefficients and computational time. This complexity did not provide any increased accuracy relative to vintage models, but it does provide business value in account management, collections, pricing, and strategic planning.

The added complexity of roll rate models when compared to time series models provided little benefit other than the chance to be more accurate for the first four months of the forecast. Vintage models were the overall winners in the accuracy versus complexity trade-off, so long as sufficient data exists for robust estimation.

In all of these calculations, the choice of the "foreseeable period" was surprisingly unimportant. Whether 12 or 36-month horizons had been used rather than the 24-month choice here, the results would have been largely the same. Starting from a lifetime loss forecast, using a time-value-of-money discounting of the projected monthly losses at the par rate on the mortgage results in a 20% to 30% decrease in the reserve amount. Estimating the principal and interest payments adjusted for the risk of default or prepayment from the loss model and then discounting with the par rate on the mortgage results in a 70% to 80% reduction in the loss reserve as compared to the original lifetime loss forecast. The magnitude of the change from the old loan loss rules to CECL will depend strongly on the lifetime of the asset and the point in the economic cycle when the adoption occurs. For 30-year fixed mortgage, the average life of loan is about 5.5 years and the lifetime loss reserve will be 4 times a historic average approach with 24 month loss emergence period. If adoption had occurred just before the onset of the last recession, the adjustment would have been $10\times$. At the peak of the recession the change would have been $2\times$. Well into recovery they would have been at parity.

If the full discounted cash flow approach is compared to the previous approach, the overall increase is only 26% through-the-cycle, with wide variations through the economic cycle, both positive and negative. By design, the new CECL rules provide a significant amount of flexibility in implementation. As seen from this study, even with a straightforward product like 30-year fixed rate conforming mortgages, the range of models listed in the CECL guidelines can produce a range of lifetime loss numbers that vary by a factor of 2. With the option of discounted cash flows, then the range of final answers would vary by a factor of 4.

Being able to choose options that will create such different answers will put the burden on lenders not only to choose the most appropriate models for their portfolios, but in doing so to also choose the level of loss via the models chosen, and to defend that choice to validators, auditors, and examiners.

2.13 What Good Is CECL?

CECL was adopted in response to the extreme mismatch between losses and loss reserves through the last economic cycle. Although trying to align the two would seem to be a benefit to lenders, it does not come without cost and disruption. Therefore, most lenders appear to be unhappy about having to adopt the new rules.

As with any new rule, the question is, what can we get from CECL? What good is a lifetime loss forecast? Some things come to mind.

Honestly, loss forecasting is a bit of an anomaly. The level of expected loss is unimportant if it is matched by revenue. Portfolio failures are not loss estimation failures. They are pricing failures. Too often lenders price by the market completely independent of their loss expectations. The clearest potential benefit of CECL is to provide a lifetime loss estimate at the time of origination, i.e. at the time of pricing. Loss estimation is a scenario-based exercise, so one cannot be certain of a loan's profitability from origination, but the loss estimation can reveal what kind of economic assumptions are required for the loan to be profitable. Invariably some segments are found to be unprofitable even under current economic conditions. Once CECL is adopted, no lender should be without a profit model by vintage.

The above assertion is true in a straightforward way for term loans. Line-of-credit are more challenging. Although a carefully chosen CECL model for lines-of-credit should be usable for profitability, the CECL loss estimate is not necessarily the correct number. Given the interpretation where future purchases are not considered for the CECL loss estimate, the number will not be appropriate for profit forecasting. However, if the model can be used with or without new purchases, then creating the necessarily lifetime loss estimate for pricing is a simple matter.

Because of the different treatment of loans and lines under CECL, portfolio managers will need to consider possibly shifting their product mix. Whereas long term loans can significantly increase loss reserves, lines-of-credit could lower reserves. Depending upon the financial metrics one is managing to, CECL will almost certainly bring a different definition of optimal to the portfolio.

PART II

Model Details

3

Historic Averages

This and following chapters provide details of the models whose results were shown previously. The goal is to provide complete visibility into the methods used so that others may confirm these results and have a starting point for the modifications and refinements necessary to meet the needs of each portfolio.

In order to assess the new, forward-looking models under CECL, the first model tested was the old, backward-looking approach. Historic average or "look-back" models performed poorly through the mortgage crisis. Otherwise FASB would not have needed to move to CECL. However, in the interest of simplicity, a number of practitioners have championed the idea of using historic averages for CECL. The results shown above make clear that a backward looking model is unfit for use in lifetime loss estimates. The discussion here shows how such models are created.

For the historic average model, in order to apply to CECL, a competing risks approach was still used. The key rates were

$$\text{Pay-off rate}(t) = \frac{\text{Pay-off balance}(t)}{\text{Outstanding balance}(t-1)} \qquad (3.1)$$

$$\text{Default rate}(t) = \frac{\text{Default balance}(t)}{\text{Outstanding balance}(t-1)} \qquad (3.2)$$

This is already an enhancement over the kind of historic average models typically used today, because they tend to consider only defaults. Including prepayments is necessary to capture the effective life of the loan.

Figures 3.1 & 3.2 show these time series segmented by risk grade. They have the expected structure, with defaults peaking after the 2009

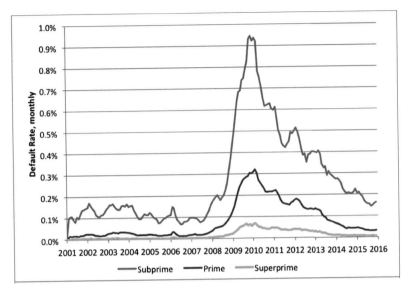

Figure 3.1. Balance default rates by risk grade.

recession stacked by risk grade. Balance pay-down has a much more dynamic structure with the most sensitivity in the superprime segments. Subprime has comparatively little opportunity to prepay or refinance, so the structure is muted.

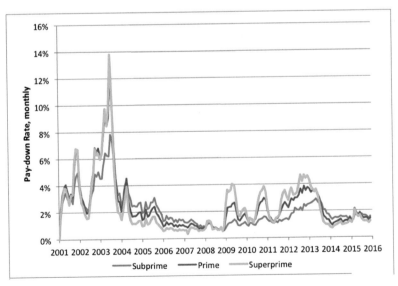

Figure 3.2. Balance pay-down rates by risk grade, includes all balance pay-ments.

For the study, a look-back period (moving average window) of 12 months was chosen. Thus, at the beginning of each forecast period, the average pay-off and default rates were computed for the previous 12 months. Twelve is not a magical answer, but it is the value most in fashion today among examiners and auditors. If one were to try to optimize the look-back period for forecast accuracy, a short value is most appropriate because the autocorrelation time of the economy tends to be around six to twelve months. By using twelve, seasonality can be ignored.

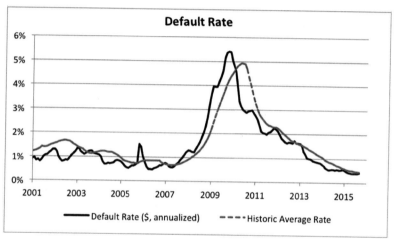

Figure 3.3. A graph of the available data showing the point-in-time balance default rate and a 12-month moving average default rate.

Figure 3.3 shows the historic default rate for the mortgage data in the study and a twelve month historic average default rate. Of course, loss reserves always lag the extremes of the economic cycle, so the reserves are never available when needed most. Also, such a simple approach continues to punish lenders for past events. The bankruptcy law change in 2006 created a short-term spike that persisted for the following year in the historic average.

4

Time Series

Most of the models developed in the DFA CECL Study include aspects of time series modeling. For model referred to here as a *the time series* model, only economic correlations of pay-down and default rates were used for the forecasting. The definition of the rates for the competing risks framework is the same as that defined in Equations 3.1 & 3.2. Lifetime losses were simulated by projecting forward under a mean-reverting base macroeconomic scenario until all currently outstanding balances were either paid-off or defaulted. Transformation of the macroeconomic data and model estimation are the primary considerations in developing the models.

Pure macroeconomic time series models necessarily assume that all portfolio dynamics are explainable by the economy. Since portfolio management actions are often correlated to economic conditions, this implies that the lender's future underwriting and account management decisions are predictable from macroeconomic scenarios based upon past actions. For the entire lending industry, previous studies suggest this may be true (Breeden and Canals-Cerdá 2016). However, this is a strong assumption for an individual lender.

4.1 Stationarity Tests

Standard practice in time series modeling is to conduct a stationarity (unit root) test prior to beginning the analysis. Several such tests are available. As an example, the Augmented Dickey-Fuller test was applied to the default rate time series in Figure 3.3 with 12 lags. Figure 4.1 shows the p-values obtained across different time spans of the data. Usually a p-value below 0.05 or 0.10 is taken as sufficient proof that the time series is stationary. The table shows that the result is highly sensitive to the time span chosen.

Data Start \ Data End	2001	2002	2003	2004	2005	2006	2007	2008	2009	2010	2011	2012	2013	2014
2001			0.09	0.74	0.71	0.66	0.78	0.99	0.90	0.17	0.09	0.14	0.30	0.32
2002				0.36	0.91	0.53	0.87	0.99	0.90	0.17	0.08	0.17	0.35	0.36
2003					0.99	0.62	0.84	0.99	0.96	0.23	0.13	0.27	0.44	0.43
2004						0.65	0.88	0.99	0.92	0.25	0.19	0.38	0.53	0.48
2005							0.99	0.99	0.52	0.19	0.28	0.44	0.54	0.43
2006								0.99	0.69	0.09	0.43	0.48	0.54	0.38
2007									0.68	0.01	0.53	0.39	0.32	0.13
2008										0.13	0.33	0.09	0.02	0.01
2009											0.58	0.04	0.01	0.01
2010												0.71	0.96	0.80
2011													0.99	0.67
2012														0.99
2013														
2014														

Figure 4.1. Estimated *p*-values from the Augmented Dickey-Fuller unit root test as applied to different ranges of the data in Figure 3.3.

If the time series is estimated to be non-stationary, standard practice is to take the first difference of the time series before creating regression models. However, modeling first differences accentuates high-frequency changes, usually caused by seasonality or changes in collections. Modeling the default rate time series directly will create an emphasis on long-term changes such as the 2009 recession. Figure 4.2 provides a visual comparison. For the differenced series, the bankruptcy law change becomes as dramatic as the recession.

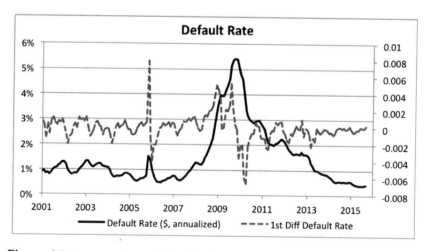

Figure 4.2. A comparison of the default rate and first difference of the default rate.

One could either truncate the data to a region that is stationary or model the differences. However, imagine that only data from 2011 onward was available. The first differences show no useful structure other than seasonality. Modeling the default rate directly would have the problem that only a recovery is seen, so they results would be very uncertain, but they would at least show a consistent trend when compared to macroeconomic factors like unemployment.

These results present a real philosophical question. Are we modeling a dataset or a process? As an industry and practitioners we know much more about the process of loan defaults than we know from the time series in Figure 3.3. Datasets are available that show the mortgage default rate back to the 1980s. Such datasets would show that default rate is not trending through time. For a given segment, default rates oscillate through the economic cycle but return to similar base levels.

Perhaps more importantly, many regulatory calculations rely on an assumption that default rates are stationary. For Basel II, a through-the-cycle (TTC) average PD must be estimated as the primary input to the capital calculation. If the default rate was not stationary, TTC PD would be undefined. Even the CECL rules allow for use of a TTC PD after the foreseeable future, which presumes that it exists.

Because must more is known about default rate as a process than just the time series available for the study, we have chosen to model the process. Therefore, all data was used without truncation and values of the default rate were regressed directly against macroeconomic factors without differencing.

4.2 Transformations

The Federal Reserve provides macroeconomic factors in the language of economists, such as quarterly percentage change in GDP. However, such transformations are poor choices for modeling. Percentage change in particular is discouraged, because it is both non-Normal and asymmetric in changes.

Asymmetry refers to the property that equivalent increases and decreases in the percentage change do not sum to zero. In other words, percentage changes are path dependent. Mathematically, we would say that percentage changes are not commutative. Table 4.1 provides a simple example of how a 20% increase in a factor like HPI, followed by a 20% decrease does not return the index to its starting value.

t	Change	Formula	Result
1	Base	$HPI(1)$	100
2	+20%	$HPI(2) = HPI(1) * 1.2$	120
3	−20%	$HPI(3) = HPI(2) * 0.8$	96

Table 4.1. Example of asymmetry in percentage changes.

Because of this asymmetry, a log-ratio transformation has long been preferred in creating forecast models, particularly in models of portfolio returns where such distinctions are critical. In the present context, the goal is simply to make certain that a linear regression model will extrapolate properly to extreme values without encountering nonlinearities or fixed boundaries because of the input factors having non-Normal distributions or being asymmetric in the changes.

Table 4.2 lists all of the preferred transformations and the less desirable transformations that they should replace.

Examples	Defined Range	Preferred Transform	Discouraged Transform
Unemployment Rate; Consumer Debt Burden	0 to 1	Log-odds	Using as is
House Price Index; GDP; CPI	0 to ∞	Log-ratio	Percentage change
Interest rates	0 to ∞	Log	Using as is
House Price Appreciation; Stock Market Returns	−1 to ∞	Revert to underlying index and apply log-ratio	Using as is
Mortgage Equity Withdrawal	−∞ to ∞	Normalize to inflation	Using as is

Table 4.2. Examples of best transformation choices for common macroeconomic variables.

Table 4.3 provides mathematical definitions of all the transformations being discussed.

4.3 Lags and Windows

To optimize the transformation of the macroeconomic factor, lags need to be considered. A change in a macroeconomic factor may not

Transformation	Input Range	Output Range	Transform Definition
Percentage Change	0 to ∞	−1 to ∞	$x(t) = (u(t) - u(t-w))/u(t-w)$
Log-odds	0 to 1	−∞ to ∞	$x_t = \log(u_t/(1 - u_t))$
Log-ratio	0 to ∞	−∞ to ∞	$x_t = \log(u(t)/u(t-w))$
Log	0 to ∞	−∞ to ∞	$x_t = \log(u_t)$

Table 4.3. Definitions of common transformations for input variable $u(t)$ to output variable $x(t)$.

immediately impact the target variable, such as a charge-off rate or pay-down rate. Rather, a lag may exist between economic shifts and loan performance. Distributed Lag Models (DLM) (Judge et al. 1985) are a standard approach to capturing lagged responses.

A DLM estimates a regression model with one coefficient relating each prior value of the explanatory (macroeconomic) factor to the target variable, as visualized in Figure 4.3

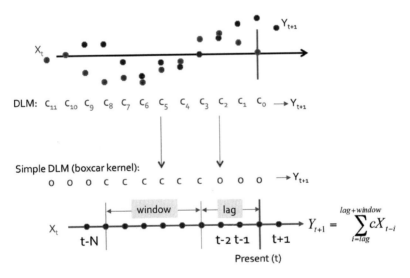

Figure 4.3. A Distributed Lag Model (DLM) as simplified to moving averages or moving changes.

Unfortunately, with only one economic cycle to model against, the potentially dozens of coefficients needed by a standard DLM cannot be estimated with stability. For this reason, practitioners employ kernels that reduce the parameter space by imposing a structure on the coefficients. The simplest possible kernel is the boxcar kernel, as illustrated in the bottom of Figure 4.3. The boxcar kernel assigns 0 coefficients to any value between 0 and "lag", then a constant coefficient between "lag" and lag + "window", and finally a 0 coefficient to any value older than lag + window. Therefore, "lag" is the time needed for an economic shock to impact the portfolio and window is the length of time that the given shock impacts the portfolio. With this structure, the DLM model is really being simplified to lagged moving averages or lagged changes, although more complex kernels could be considered as more historic data is accumulated.

For a moving average transformation, the range being averaged is the window. For example, a 12-month moving average would have a window of 12. The lag refers to how far into the past the values are taken for computing the moving average. When the regression model is estimated, a single coefficient is applied to macroeconomic factor after transformation with lag and window. For change transformations such as log-ratio, the window specifies the span over which the change is computed.

All of the transformations described in Table 4.3 can include the option for lags and windows. Also, lag and window can be used in combination, so "Unemployment rate, Moving average: L 6 W 12" means that a moving average of the unemployment rate is computed with a 12-month window, all lagged by 6 months.

4.4 Factor Selection

Explanatory factors (macroeconomic factors) must be selected from the available data and appropriate transformations chosen. For the current study, only factors available in the DFAST datasets were considered, so that scenarios would be available. Further, only factors close to the consumer's finances were considered. For example, although exchange rates might be indicative of trends in the economy, they impact consumers only indirectly through such factors as interest rates, GDP, and unemployment.

This pattern has been observed globally. Regardless of the cause of a recession, consumers are always impacted by factors such as unemployment, house prices, wages, and debt service burden. Even the Hong Kong SARS recession of 2002 is a case in point. Although default rates correlated well to hospital admissions, equally accurate models could be created using unemployment rates and house prices. The benefit of focusing on factors close to the consumer is that the resulting model can generalize to many types of recession.

Considering all this, Table 4.4 shows the list of factors available in the DFAST scenarios that were considered for this study. The Dow Jones Industrial Average (DJIA) is a marginal choice given the above logic. It should have little effect on subprime and even most prime consumers, but was worth testing in case some sensitivity is present for superprime consumers, assuming a correlation between consumer assets in equities and credit risk.

Variable	Transformation
Disposable Personal Income (DPI)	Log ratio
Unemployment rate	Moving average
Unemployment rate	Difference
Unemployment rate	Log ratio
House Price Index (HPI)	Log ratio
Mortgage Interest rate	Difference
Real GDP	Log ratio
DJIA	Log ratio

Table 4.4. Variables and transformations tested for correlation to the default rate and pay-down rate time series.

Just as stationarity was discussed for the default rate, stationarity of the macroeconomic factors should also be considered. In the case of default rate, industry experience is that default rate does not trend over decades and is not an integrated series. The same cannot be said for all macroeconomic factors. GDP, even in real terms is an integrated series that trends strongly through time. So to is the HPI. If they were used without transformation, it would build a bias into out-of-sample forecasts. Therefore the preferred approach is to use a log-ratio transformation with these series.

Unemployment rate is essential to any consumer default rate model and yet presents many challenges. Generally, consumers do not default the moment they lose their jobs, and an economic measure of unemployment is not a specific indicator that borrowers in the portfolio have lost their jobs. Rather default occurs when consumers no longer have the income or assets necessary to pay their bills. In non-recessionary periods the lag between unemployment and default rate is typically about six months. However, in times of economic stress, the government can increase the duration unemployment benefits to cushion the blow to consumers. In the 2009 recession, benefits were increased to 99 weeks (about 24 months). Interestingly, estimates of the lag between unemployment and default using data from the 2009 recession often come in around 24 months.

Obviously, for unemployment more than any other factor, lag is really a function of the phase of the economy, but we perpetually lack sufficient data to create such asymmetric models. Instead, examiners tend to impose a limit on lagged responses of 12 months with the goal of seeing a more immediate response between stressed scenarios and portfolio performance. Although CECL is not about stress testing, the same limits were kept as a reasonable compromise between calm and stressed macroeconomic periods.

Given these challenges, practitioners have not concluded which transformation is best for unemployment. In some datasets, moving averages are best. Other datasets show changes in unemployment rate to be most predictive. Some models even include both simultaneously. The choice is not a matter of stationarity, but rather a question of what drives defaults and is tangled with the changing unemployment benefits. In the current study, several transforms are considered and the optimization process will choose.

A better measure than unemployment would be to measure changes in all consumer income, including all benefits such as unemployment, health care, pensions, etc. Such measures probably exist, but are not in the DFAST scenarios, so unemployment rate is the proxy.

All of the data selection and transformation decisions are based upon the long history of the macroeconomic data. If only macroeconomic data overlapping the available default rate time series were tested, the same unstable stationarity test results would occur as shown in Figure 4.1. Instead, if data is tested back to the late 1980s, all of these will test as stationary. This time span was chosen based upon autocorrelation studies of macroeconomic data and the nature of recessions. In the late 1980s US monetary policy changed with a corresponding change in the rate and structure of entering and exiting recessions (Taylor 1999).

4.5 Model Estimation Process

For each key rate that is being modeled with macroeconomic factors, default rate and prepayment rate for this model, the transformations for those factors need to be optimized. Univariate optimizations were conducted for each macroeconomic factor to optimize the lag and window for the chosen transformation. The best such univariate models were selected and combined to a final multifactor regression model.

This two-step process of first optimizing the individual macroeconomic factor transformations and then creating a multifactor regression model is employed, because a single-step optimization would require a nonlinear search across a landscape with many local optima. The approach employed here cannot guarantee a global optimum, but it reduces overfitting and focuses the result on explaining the dominant events (recessions). As part of this process, any result with the wrong sign for the correlation is rejected, e.g. if rising unemployment predicted falling defaults, we assume an erroneous result was obtained due to data noise.

For each rate, the macroeconomic model will have the form

$$\tilde{r}(t) = \sum_{j=1}^{N} c_j T\Big(E_j(t); \text{transform}_j, \text{lag}_j, \text{window}_j\Big) \qquad (4.1)$$

where transform, lag, and window were separately optimized for each macroeconomic factor j, and the coefficients c_j come from the linear regression algorithm.

4.6 Autocorrelated Residuals and Autoregressive Terms

Standard industry practice is to conduct a Durbin-Watson test (Durbin and Watson 1950) on the monthly model residuals to test for autocorrelation. If residual autocorrelation is found, then the estimated coefficients will be correct, but the confidence intervals and p-values for the coefficients will be incorrect.

Unfortunately, the Durbin-Watson test itself does not apply when lagged dependent variables are included in the model, such as will be the case through all of the models in the study. The Breusch-Godfrey Lagrange multiplier (BGLM) test (Breusch 1978, Godfrey 1978) should instead be used to test for serial correlation in the residuals when lagged macroeconomic factors are included.

However, the test does not need to be performed, because the models are already expected to fail any test of autocorrelation. The residuals will be autocorrelated, because loan performance is not fully explainable by macroeconomic factors. The divergences are often caused by portfolio management changes, which span periods of time that create autocorrelated residuals. Data on policy changes are generally not available to model and are not available in the current mortgage data.

Therefore, the model development proceeds on the assumption that the residuals will be correlated, Some practitioners add autoregressive (AR) or moving average (MA) terms to the models, the goal being to eliminate the residual autocorrelation, but at the risk of changing the model estimation with AR terms or ambiguity with MA terms when forecasting multiple periods into the future.

Instead, the current study leaves the regression equation unchanged but performs robust error estimation in order to estimate confidence intervals and p-values even though the residuals are assumed to be auto-correlated. Although the Newey-West estimator theoretically resolves some of the problems in the standard estimator, practical experience has shown uncertainty in the Newey-West uncertainty estimates. There is no perfect answer. Judgment is still required.

For all of the reported results, a Newey-West algorithm is employed to estimate confidence intervals and p-values.

4.7 National Model Coefficients

The above approach was applied to the data in Figures 3.1 & 3.2 where each macroeconomic factor was optimized independently, then all possible combinations were tried. Any model with insignificant p-values, signs that flipped relative to industry intuition, or high variance inflation factors (VIF) were rejected.

AIC	Factors	
1459.5	Unemployment.rate.MovingAvg	House.Price.Index.LogRatio
1577.444	Real.GDP.LogRatio	Unemployment.rate.MovingAvg
1753.81	Real.DPI.LogRatio	Unemployment.rate.MovingAvg
1851.127	Unemployment.rate.MovingAvg	
2347.065	House.Price.Index.LogRatio	
5779.966	Real.GDP.LogRatio	
6820.122	Unemployment.rate.LogRatio	
8191.199	Unemployment.rate.Diff	
11611.44	Real.DPI.LogRatio	

Table 4.5. A ranking of candidate models by AIC that satisfy the sign and p-value constraints. Combinations of up to four macroeconomic factors were searched, but only these satisfied the constraints.

At the end of that process, Table 4.5 has the candidate models obtained for the subprime segment. They are ranked by the Akaike Information Criterion (AIC), which provides a relative measure of accuracy adjusted for the model complexity. From these candidates, the most predictive uses unemployment and house prices, which is no surprise.

Table 4.6 lists the regression statistics provided for each model. The regression statistics for the best model are shown in Table 4.7.

Output	Definition
Estimate c_j	The estimated coefficient for the factor's contribution to the model.
Standard Coefficient	The relative importance of the factor to the model, $sc_j = c_j * sd_j / sd_y$ for linear regression $sc_j = \sqrt{3}/\pi * sd_j * c_j$ for binomial regression where sd is the standard deviation
Standard Error se_j	The uncertainty in the estimated coefficient
t-Value	The significance of the estimate in units of the standard error
$Pr(> |t|)$	The probability of randomly obtaining the observed coefficient

Table 4.6. Regression output definitions

Table 4.7 has the estimates for subprime balance default rate. The standardized coefficients measure the sensitivity of the model to the various factors. Clearly house prices comprise most of the model dynamics.

This model includes dummy variables for month of the year (seasonality) and the two best macroeconomic factors. January was chosen as a reference level for the seasonality estimates. Note that p-values should not be interpreted individually for the levels of a single variable like seasonality, because the reference level is arbitrary and the p-values simply indicate whether the estimate is close to the reference level. If all seasonal dummies had large p-values, then one would conclude that collectively seasonality was unimportant. Instead, these results show that seasonality is nonzero for some months. If the intercept term was excluded from the estimate it would be picked up in the seasonal coefficients thereby making the p-values strongly significant for all months. That would just be an artifact of estimation. One must be very careful in interpreting p-values.

Goodness of fit is less straight-forward to measure for logistic regression models, because the usual R^2 measure is not defined. AIC was used for model selection, but AIC is a relative measure whose absolute value

Factor	Estimate	Std Coeff	Std. Error	z value	$Pr(> |z|)$
(Intercept)	−7.608		0.0677	−112.4	< 2e-16
Jan	0	0			
Feb	0.043	0.082	0.0230	1.9	0.061
Mar	0.037	0.038	0.0230	1.6	0.109
Apr	−0.031	−0.006	0.0234	−1.3	0.183
May	−0.083	−0.159	0.0237	−3.5	4.6E-04
Jun	−0.139	−0.143	0.0241	−5.8	7.9E-09
Jul	−0.141	−0.028	0.0241	−5.9	4.6E-09
Aug	−0.171	−0.326	0.0243	−7.0	2.1E-12
Sep	−0.123	−0.127	0.0240	−5.1	2.6E-07
Oct	−0.098	−0.019	0.0238	−4.1	3.6E-05
Nov	−0.028	−0.054	0.0234	−1.2	0.224
Dec	−0.005	−0.005	0.0232	−0.2	0.830
Unemployment.rate lwMovingAvg.L0.W1	0.262	0.051	0.0091	28.9	< 2e-16
House.Price.Index lwLogRatio.L12.W24	−0.533	−1.018	0.0468	−11.4	< 2e-16

Table 4.7. Coefficients are shown for the model of subprime balance default rate. January was set as the reference level for the seasonality coefficients. Pseudo $R^2 = 0.97$

is not particularly interesting. One common alternative is to report

$$\text{pseudo } R^2 = 1 - \frac{\text{Residual Deviance}}{\text{Null Deviance}} \tag{4.2}$$

Expected values of pseudo R^2 change dramatically just based upon the level of aggregation in the data, as will be seen with the loan-level models later.

As described earlier, Table 4.7 contains the standard p-values, which are biased toward being overly optimistic for auto-correlated residuals, meaning that the uncertainties look smaller than they really are. Table 4.8 contains the regression output with Newey-West error estimates. Generally the Newey-West p-values are higher (less certainty that the estimates are non-zero) both for this model and most models of default rates.

Generalized variance inflation factors (GVIF) were estimated to measure the extent of multicolinearity problems in the estimates. The variance inflation factor compares the measured standard error to what it would be if the variable were uncorrelated with the other variables.

Factor	Estimate	Std Coeff	Std. Error	z value	$Pr(> \lvert z \rvert)$
(Intercept)	−7.608		0.3050	−24.9432	< 2.2e-16
Jan	0.000	0			
Feb	0.043	0.082	0.0160	2.689	0.007
Mar	0.037	0.038	0.0335	1.1006	0.271
Apr	−0.031	−0.006	0.0291	−1.0728	0.283
May	−0.083	−0.159	0.0362	−2.2941	0.022
Jun	−0.139	−0.143	0.0464	−2.9883	0.003
Jul	−0.141	−0.028	0.0429	−3.29	0.001
Aug	−0.171	−0.326	0.0459	−3.716	2.0E-04
Sep	−0.123	−0.127	0.0517	−2.3849	0.017
Oct	−0.098	−0.019	0.0271	−3.6339	2.8E-04
Nov	−0.028	−0.054	0.0328	−0.8661	0.386
Dec	−0.005	−0.005	0.0493	−0.1014	0.919
Unemployment.rate lwMovingAvg.L0.W1	0.262	0.051	0.0428	6.1324	8.7E-10
House.Price.Index lwLogRatio.L12.W24	−0.533	−1.018	0.1933	−2.7543	0.006

Table 4.8. Multivariate model for subprime mortgage balance default rate with Newey-West coefficients.

The square root is usually reported, but no firm rule exists for how high is too high.

Factor	GVIF	Df	$GVIF^{1/(2*Df)}$
Seasonality	1.005361	11	1.000243
Unemployment.rate.lwMovingAvg.L0.W1	9.531163	1	3.087258
House.Price.Index.lwLogRatio.L12.W24	9.532158	1	3.087419

Table 4.9. Variance inflation factors for the subprime model.

Table 4.9 shows the GVIF values for the subprime model. Seasonality is apparently uncorrelated with the other factors, but the colinearity between unemployment and HPI causes an inflation in the error estimates of 3×. Although fixed rules exist, this is below most commonly suggested values.

Factor	Estimate	Std Coeff	Std. Error	z value	$Pr(>|z|)$
(Intercept)	−10.469		0.220	−47.52	< 2e-16
Jan	0	0			
Feb	0.041	0.078	0.020	2.05	0.040
Mar	0.040	0.041	0.044	0.90	0.368
Apr	−0.027	−0.052	0.036	−0.77	0.442
May	−0.070	−0.072	0.046	−1.53	0.125
Jun	−0.108	−0.206	0.062	−1.73	0.084
Jul	−0.114	−0.118	0.047	−2.41	0.016
Aug	−0.132	−0.252	0.057	−2.31	0.021
Sep	−0.120	−0.123	0.065	−1.83	0.067
Oct	−0.106	−0.203	0.041	−2.57	0.010
Nov	−0.067	−0.069	0.049	−1.38	0.169
Dec	−0.053	−0.101	0.061	−0.87	0.382
Unemployment.rate lwMovingAvg.L0.W1	0.479	0.493	0.025	19.11	< 2e-16

Table 4.10. Multivariate Model for prime mortgage balance default rate with Newey-West Coefficients.

GVIF is not shown for the prime and superprime models, because only a single macroeconomic factor appears in each, and that if again found to be uncorrelated with seasonality.

Factor	Estimate	Std Coeff	Std. Error	z value	$Pr(>|z|)$
(Intercept)	−12.488		0.306	−40.86	< 2.2e-16
Jan	0	0			
Feb	0.079	0.150	0.037	2.14	0.032
Mar	0.063	0.064	0.039	1.62	0.105
Apr	0.018	0.034	0.041	0.44	0.660
May	−0.046	−0.047	0.036	−1.29	0.197
Jun	−0.046	−0.088	0.050	−0.91	0.362
Jul	−0.047	−0.048	0.046	−1.03	0.305
Aug	−0.047	−0.091	0.048	−1.00	0.319
Sep	−0.034	−0.035	0.063	−0.54	0.587
Oct	−0.099	−0.189	0.032	−3.10	0.002
Nov	−0.045	−0.047	0.029	−1.57	0.117
Dec	−0.054	−0.103	0.047	−1.14	0.252
Unemployment.rate lwMovingAvg.L0.W2	0.527	0.541	0.034	15.56	< 2.2e-16

Table 4.11. Multivariate Model for superprime mortgage balance default rate with Newey-West Coefficients.

Following the same process for the prime and superprime segments, the final results are given in Tables 4.10 & 4.11. These results show only the Newey-West error estimates. Note that in both cases, the best model by the AIC criterion was a univariate unemployment rate model, even with the same lag and window parameters.

The seasonality estimates are interesting to compare. Figure 4.4 shows the estimates for subprime, prime, and superprime. The three estimates broadly agree, showing the Christmas season deterioration and tax refund season recoveries, although superprime is less dynamic. January is used as the reference level, so all three functions start at 0. No explanation is immediately obvious for the convergence of estimates in October.

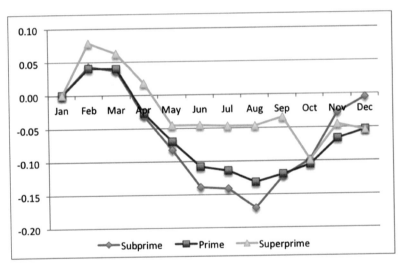

Figure 4.4. A comparison of seasonality coefficients for subprime, prime, and superprime for the balance default rate models. The coefficients are in units of log-odds of default.

The results for the balance pay-down modeling are given in Tables 4.12–4.14. The results are displayed in the same format as for the balance default rate.

Factor	Estimate	Std Coeff	Std. Error	z value	$Pr(>|z|)$
(Intercept)	−5.093		0.188	−27.11	< 2.2e-16
Jan	0	0			
Feb	0.030	0.057	0.030	0.98	0.326
Mar	0.133	0.003	0.041	3.21	1.3E-03
Apr	0.144	0.140	0.043	3.34	8.4E-04
May	0.171	0.008	0.060	2.87	4.1E-03
Jun	0.139	0.265	0.060	2.32	0.020
Jul	0.138	0.003	0.056	2.45	0.014
Aug	0.129	0.126	0.048	2.67	7.7E-03
Sep	0.036	0.002	0.041	0.88	0.379
Oct	0.123	0.235	0.034	3.66	2.5E-04
Nov	0.042	0.001	0.045	0.93	0.355
Dec	0.105	0.103	0.053	1.98	0.047
Real.DPI lwLogRatio.L12.W24	2.191	0.103	0.930	2.35	0.019
Unemployment.rate lwMovingAvg.L12.W24	0.084	0.160	0.025	3.40	6.6E-04
House.Price.Index lwLogRatio.L0.W6	2.321	0.055	0.602	3.85	1.2E-04

Table 4.12. Multivariate Model for subprime mortgage balance pay-down rate with Newey-West Coefficients.

Factor	Estimate	Std Coeff	Std. Error	z value	$Pr(>|z|)$
(Intercept)	−5.310		0.373	−14.25	< 2.2e-16
Jan	0	0			
Feb	0.033	0.064	0.080	0.41	0.680
Mar	0.144	0.059	0.077	1.88	0.061
Apr	0.103	0.099	0.073	1.39	0.163
May	0.098	0.188	0.086	1.14	0.255
Jun	0.100	0.041	0.084	1.19	0.233
Jul	0.048	0.047	0.068	0.72	0.473
Aug	0.014	0.026	0.074	0.18	0.855
Sep	−0.031	−0.013	0.071	−0.43	0.664
Oct	0.075	0.073	0.066	1.14	0.253
Nov	0.031	0.060	0.071	0.44	0.662
Dec	0.090	0.037	0.069	1.31	0.190
Mortgage.rate lwDiff.L2.W24	−0.385	−0.371	0.082	−4.71	2.46E-06
Unemployment.rate lwMovingAvg.L10.W24	0.140	0.271	0.060	2.34	0.019

Table 4.13. Multivariate Model for prime mortgage balance pay-down rate with Newey-West Coefficients.

Factor	Estimate	Std Coeff	Std. Error	z value	$Pr(> |z|)$
(Intercept)	−4.397		0.093	−47.22	< 2.2e-16
Jan	0	0			
ssnFeb	0.008	0.015	0.042	0.18	0.86
ssnMar	0.078	0.031	0.076	1.03	0.30
ssnApr	−0.013	−0.001	0.103	−0.12	0.90
ssnMay	−0.002	−0.003	0.120	−0.02	0.99
ssnJun	0.039	0.015	0.101	0.38	0.70
ssnJul	−0.041	−0.004	0.118	−0.35	0.73
ssnAug	−0.123	−0.234	0.152	−0.81	0.42
ssnSep	−0.133	−0.053	0.145	−0.91	0.36
ssnOct	0.084	0.008	0.114	0.73	0.46
ssnNov	0.004	0.008	0.117	0.03	0.97
ssnDec	0.011	0.004	0.097	0.11	0.91
Mortgage.rate lwDiff.L1.W23	−0.702	−0.064	0.133	−5.28	1.3E-07
DowJones.stock.market lwLogRatio.L0.W3	0.569	1.087	0.332	1.72	0.09

Table 4.14. Multivariate Model for superprime mortgage balance prepayment rate with Newey-West Coefficients.

For all of the multivariate prepayment models, Tables 4.12 – 4.14, the VIF estimates were 1.5 or less, meaning that the macroeconomic factors were much less correlated than for the default rate modeling.

The seasonality estimates largely agree between risk segments, Figure 4.5. The seeming parallel shift is most likely noise in the January estimates (captured in the intercepts), but the shapes of the functions are largely similar. Prepayment seasonality is roughly the opposite of the default rate seasonality, which makes sense.

4.8 In-sample Fits

Figures 4.6 & 4.7 show the in-sample fits of the balance default rate and pay-down rate using macroeconomic factors. The extrapolations are made using the base, adverse, and severe DFAST scenarios.

Visually macroeconomic factors can be used to explain the variation in balance default rates, although we learn in later models that some of this is spurious correlation that is more appropriately explained with

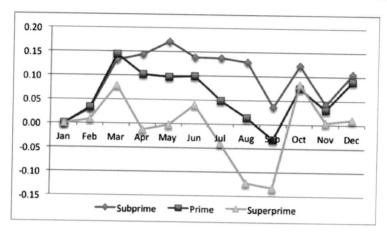

Figure 4.5. A comparison of seasonality coefficients for subprime, prime, and superprime for the balance prepayment rate models. The coefficients are in units of log-odds of default.

other factors. The balance pay-down rates are more difficult to explain with macroeconomic factors alone.

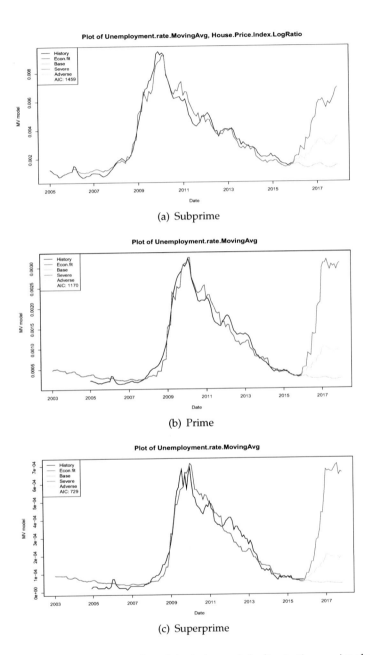

(a) Subprime

(b) Prime

(c) Superprime

Figure 4.6. Macroeconomic fits of the balance default rate time series showing the in-sample fit and extrapolation under the three DFAST economic scenarios: base, adverse, and severe.

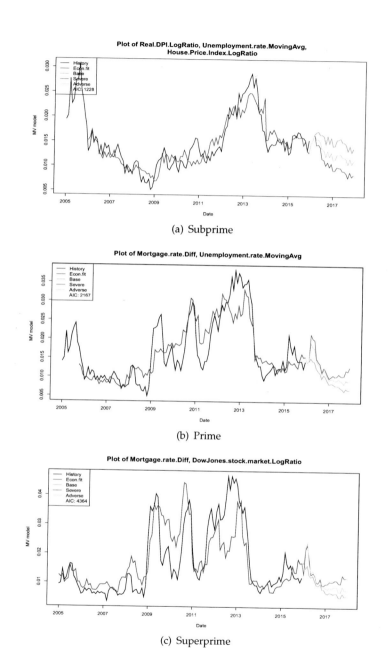

(a) Subprime

(b) Prime

(c) Superprime

Figure 4.7. Macroeconomic fits of the balance pay-down rate time series showing the in-sample fit and extrapolation under the three DFAST economic scenarios: base, adverse, and severe.

4.9 State-level Model

With 52 states and territories times 3 risk grades, the 156 models each for default rate and payment rate are too much to list here. To visualize the results, Figures 4.8 & 4.9 summarize the primary macroeconomic

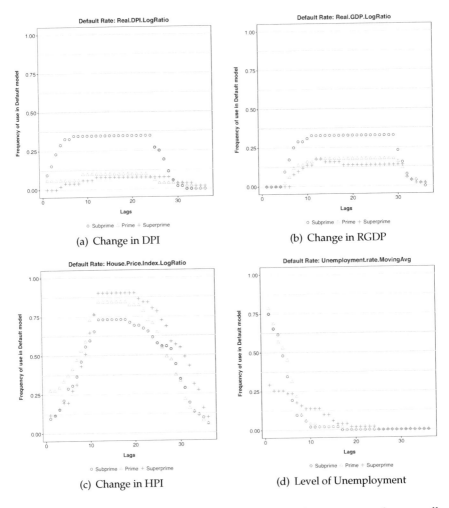

Figure 4.8. Macroeconomic dependencies for default rate averaged across all state-level and risk grade models.

sensitivities across all those models. Each figure shows the frequency that specific lagged values of the state-level macroeconomic factors are included across all the corresponding state-level models. Although each model uses a "boxcar kernel" that results from simple lags and win-

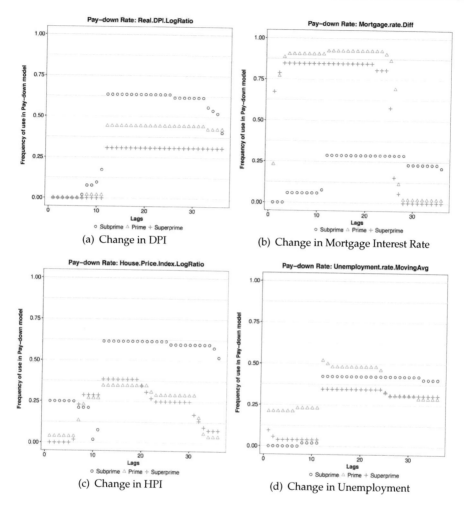

Figure 4.9. Macroeconomic dependencies for prepayment rate averaged across all state-level and risk grade models.

dows, these averages give an idea of what the full Distributed Lag Model (DLM) structure might be.

For modeling default rate, Figure 4.8, house price changes between 12 and 24 months ago were the most frequently used. Recent values of unemployment were second most important. DPI and GDP appeared in about a third of all models. Other candidate factors rarely appeared. Interestingly, disposable personal income was most important for subprime, and unemployment was noticeably less important for superprime.

For modeling prepayment rate, Figure 4.9, change in the mortgage interest rate over the previous year was most predictive, suggesting the opportunity for refinance. Also important were change in DPI, change in HPI, and moving averages of unemployment. Note that change in mortgage interest rates was unimportant for subprime, presumably because they do not qualify for refinancing. Unemployment was again unimportant for superprime.

All of these results for both default rate and prepayment rate make good intuitive sense.

4.10 Possible Enhancements

Although the mortgage database has a very large number of loans, the length in terms of economic cycles is quite short. Recessions began in March 2001 and December 2007 with subsequent unemployment peaks in June 2003 and October 2009. Figure 4.10 shows the historic unemployment rate along with a method Breeden (2014) for quantifying the number of cycles, which is not the same as the number of recessions. Recessions are declared through a formal process, but modelers need to know if a time series has useful structure regardless of whether any recessions were declared.

The middle graph of Figure 4.10 shows the phase of the economy: contracting (first quadrant), expanding (third quadrant), or transitions between the two (second and fourth quadrants). This shows that 2015 also showed a pause in the post-recession expansion, which is observed in the performance of many portfolios.

The bottom graph of Figure 4.10 shows the incremental information gained each quarter measured in economic cycles. Using a severity-weighted measure of number of cycles indicates that the data is equivalent to 2.3 economic cycles relative to the available history in this study.

With so little time history, compromises must be made in order to limit the number of coefficients being estimated. That said, some may find the approach described above of optimizing univariate window-lag transformations and then creating multifactor models to be overly restrictive. Here are some possible enhancements.

The graphs in Figures 4.8 & 4.9 suggest that instead of a boxcar kernel, a pulse shape with inverse hyperbolic tangent functions on either end might be a better fit. This allows for some imprecision in the onset and end of the crisis. The number of parameters needed for each mac-

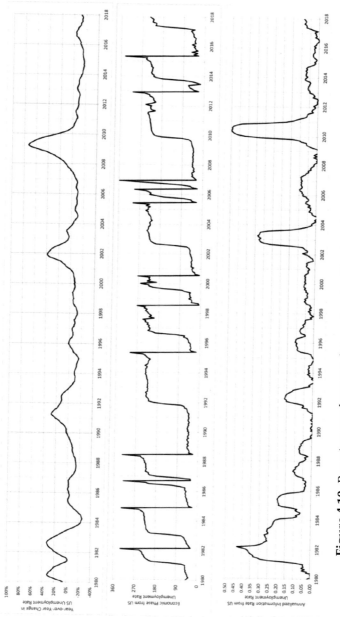

Figure 4.10. Recent unemployment data and a visualization of measuring economic cycles.

roeconomic factor would double to four by adding slow coefficients in the arc tanh functions.

Also, instead of creating 52 fully independent models, a single model could be created to simultaneously model the 52 states and territories using local economic conditions and fixed effects by state. The argument in favor of such models is that the diversity of the states raises the amount of data being modeled. In actuality, US states are highly correlated with mostly minor divergences in magnitude and timing. Experience has shown that this approach is better than a single national model but less accurate than 52 independent models. Perhaps, though, the group modeling should be used just on states on smaller states to improve the accuracy where the data is limited.

Perhaps the greatest limitation of the approach here is that each factor is independently optimized to predict the recession before combining the optimized factors. This was done because the multicolinearity between factors and the plethora of local optima when the optimization is unconstrained. A compromise would be to create the model as done here, but then perform an annealing on the window and lag coefficients to enhance the model a bit without violating the constraints on allowed signs, etc.

5

Roll Rate Models

In contrast to the time series model that considered only two outcomes (default or prepayment), roll rate models focus on the intermediate transitions through the delinquency states to default. The standard for loss forecasting in retail loan portfolios for several decades, roll rate models capture relative proportions of accounts or balances in successive delinquency buckets.

If a borrower fails to make a monthly payment, the loan will roll forward by one delinquency bucket. If instead the borrower makes a payment covering all due balances, the loan can cure to "current", synonymous with being zero days past due. However, borrowers can make partial payments, so a loan in any delinquency state can cure back to any previous delinquency state. Similarly, a previously submitted check may bounce, so a loan can jump any number of states forward.

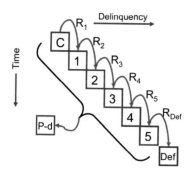

Figure 5.1. Illustration of the roll rate structure.

Roll rates are the net rates across all such possible transitions, Figure 5.1. A net roll rate combines all possible transitions to a simple ratio of accounts in bucket i at time t to accounts in the previous bucket $i-1$

in the previous month $t - 1$, Equation 5.1. Net roll rates can be defined using accounts or balances.

$$r_i(t) = \frac{\text{Balance}_i(t)}{\text{Balance}_{i-1}(t-1)} \tag{5.1}$$

To create a forecast, models must be created for each of the net roll rate time series. Many approaches could be used. For example, each roll could be split by vintage and modeled as will be done in the vintage model. In the current study, the common, simpler approach is taken where each time series is modeled with the same methodology described above for the time series model.

The roll rates in Figures 5.2 – 5.4 show the usual structure. Each successive roll has a higher rate, meaning that an account 3 months delinquent has a higher probability of going to four months delinquent than an account 2 months delinquent has of going to 3 months delinquent, for example.

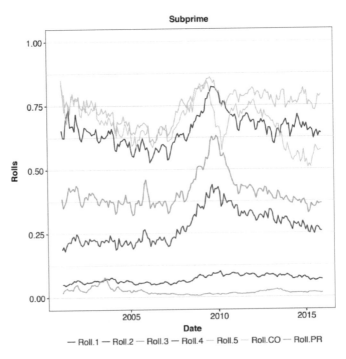

Figure 5.2. Time series of the roll rates for the national subprime segment.

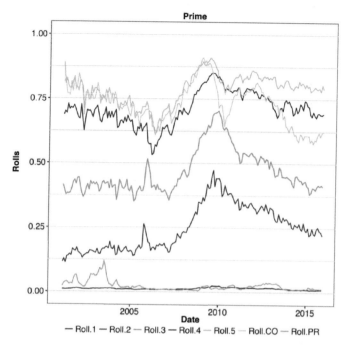

Figure 5.3. Time series of the roll rates for the national prime segment.

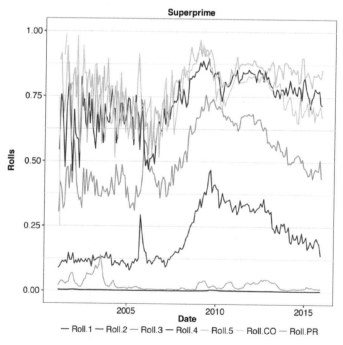

Figure 5.4. Time series of the roll rates for the national superprime segment.

As described for the earlier models, the roll rate model is only being used to model through 6 months delinquent, which is defined as default. The charge-off process for mortgage is significantly more complex, possibly with multiple partial charge-offs. Any balance dynamics past bucket 6 are being considered here as part of the recovery process, for which a constant level is assumed. Detailed modeling of partial charge-offs is outside the scope of the current project and probably beyond the scope of what one would need to implement for CECL.

5.1 Model Coefficients

Since many more models are needed for the roll rates than for the time series model, Table 5.1 has a summary view of all the models. Several patterns emerge when looking across these models. House Price Index is consistently important, and the optimal lag and window values are quite large. Note that for policy reasons, the maximum lag was 12 and the maximum window was 24. Clearly, HPI has a long-term impact on delinquency.

Unemployment was present in some form through most of the rolls, though more important for subprime and prime. Superprime only showed sensitivity for roll 1. There was a much greater diversity of optimal transformation for unemployment, probably owing to the challenges in unemployment measurement described in Section 4.4.

GDP appears in a few places, but this is mostly an indirect measure. It appears most likely through correlation with other factors that for statistical noise did not appear.

For payment rate, the models are the same as in the time series model. For prime and superprime this is driven primarily by changes in mortgage interest rates. For subprime, refinancing is not generally an option, so prepayment is more likely to be a forced sale and therefore correlated to economic stresses like unemployment.

Figures 5.2-5.4 show that even the later rolls are well resolved. The resulting models in Table 5.1 are both statistically and intuitively reasonable. In single-institution datasets, the results are not usually so well behaved. Typically rolls 4 and above are sufficiently noisy that reasonable models cannot be created. In those cases, simple moving averages are generally harmless. Having detailed models of the early roll rates will capture the dominant portfolio structure.

Variable	Segment	Intercept	Real GDP LogRatio Lag/Win	Coeff	Real DPI LogRatio Lag/Win	Coeff	Unemployment rate MovingAvg LogRatio Lag/Win	Coeff	Unemployment rate LogRatio Lag/Win	Coeff	HPI LogRatio Lag/Win	Coeff
Roll 1	Subprime	−3.179					L0.W3	0.099				
Roll 1	Prime	−4.897					L0.W1	0.100				
Roll 1	Superprime	−6.000							L5.W24	0.570	L12.W24	−0.312
Roll 2	Subprime	−1.058	L5.W24	−1.052			L0.W1	0.046			L11.W24	−0.399
Roll 2	Prime	−1.456					L0.W1	0.081			L12.W23	−0.359
Roll 2	Superprime	−2.370					L0.W1	0.179			L12.W24	−0.623
Roll 3	Subprime	−0.264									L12.W24	−0.435
Roll 3	Prime	0.045							L7.W12	1.103	L11.W18	−0.286
Roll 3	Superprime	−0.293	L5.W24	−2.989					L3.W24	0.484	L11.W21	−0.612
Roll 4	Subprime	0.484					L0.W1	0.091			L12.W24	−0.668
Roll 4	Prime	0.725					L0.W1	0.062			L9.W24	−0.738
Roll 4	Superprime	1.282					L0.W1	0.048			L12.W24	−1.077
Roll 5	Subprime	1.242									L11.W24	−0.695
Roll 5	Prime	1.482									L8.W24	−0.903
Roll 5	Superprime	1.735									L8.W24	−1.142
Roll to Def	Subprime	0.952	L0.W11	−4.711								
Roll to Def	Prime	1.086							L0.W6	3.838	L3.W23	−0.545
Roll to Def	Superprime	1.522	L0.W12	−6.428							L5.W24	−0.693

Table 5.1. Summary table for all of the macroeconomic factors used to explain the various roll rates. Lags and windows refer to parameters used in the transformations, as described in Section 4.3. Constraints were imposed on the maximum values for lags and windows of 12 and 24 respectively.

5.2 In-sample Fits

Figures 5.5 – 5.10 show the in-sample fits of macroeconomic data to the roll rates. The extrapolations show possible outcomes under the DFAST base, adverse, and severe scenarios. The fits to the early rolls are quite good, but they get weaker toward the later rolls. The second delinquency and default peak in 2012, most notable for superprime, appears to be particularly difficult to capture with economics. The roll to default captures the first peak in 2009 well, but the second one not at all.

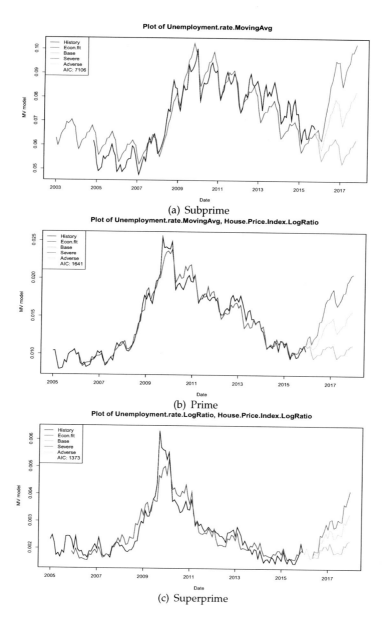

Figure 5.5. Macroeconomic fits of the roll to bucket 1 showing the in-sample fit and extrapolation under the three DFAST economic scenarios: base, adverse, and severe.

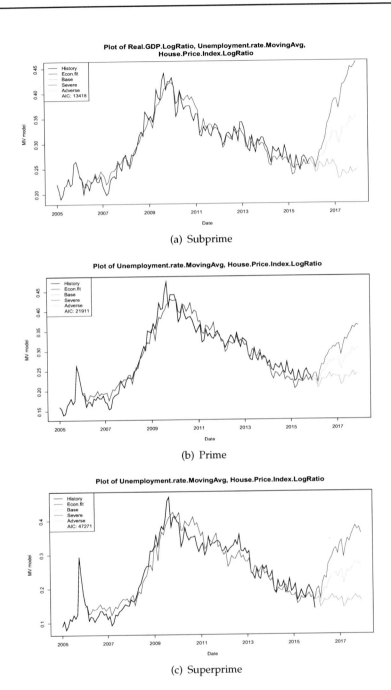

Figure 5.6. Macroeconomic fits of the roll to bucket 2 showing the in-sample fit and extrapolation under the three DFAST economic scenarios: base, adverse, and severe.

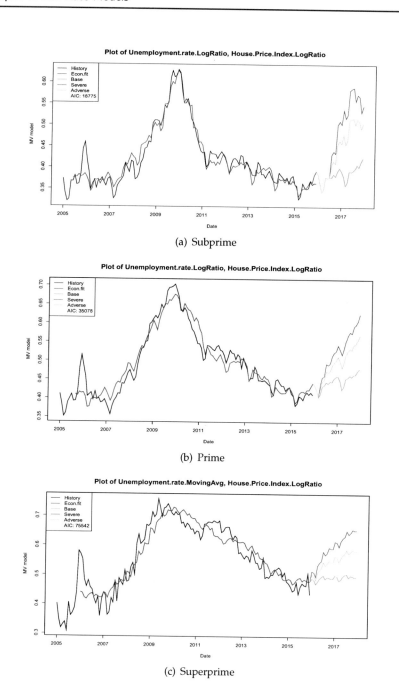

(a) Subprime

(b) Prime

(c) Superprime

Figure 5.7. Macroeconomic fits of the roll to bucket 3 showing the in-sample fit and extrapolation under the three DFAST economic scenarios: base, adverse, and severe.

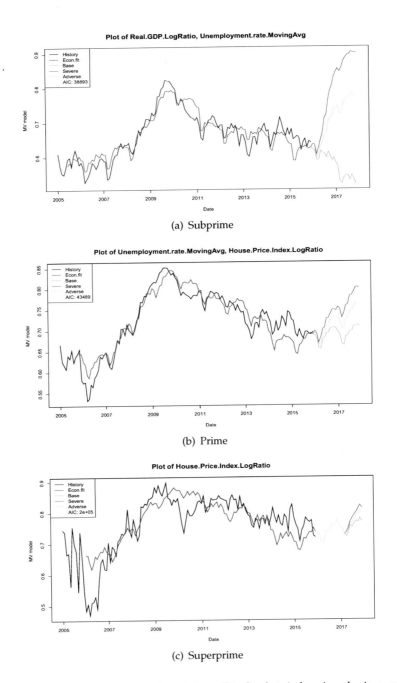

Figure 5.8. Macroeconomic fits of the roll to bucket 4 showing the in-sample fit and extrapolation under the three DFAST economic scenarios: base, adverse, and severe.

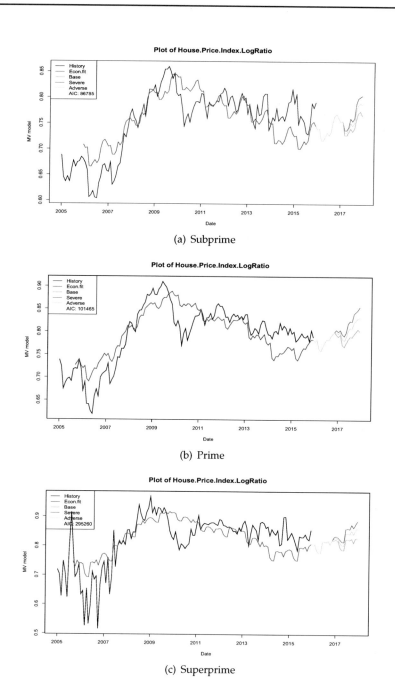

Figure 5.9. Macroeconomic fits of the roll to bucket 5 showing the in-sample fit and extrapolation under the three DFAST economic scenarios: base, adverse, and severe.

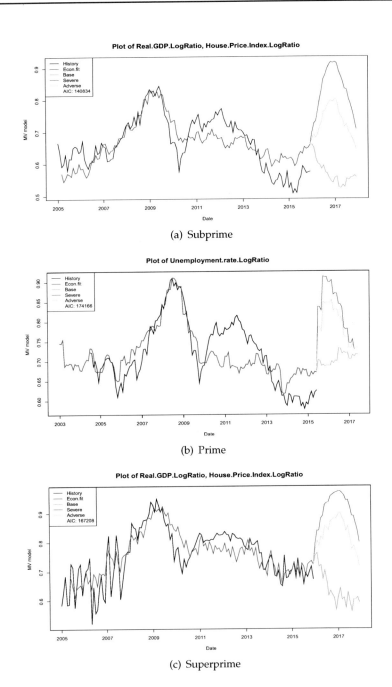

(a) Subprime

(b) Prime

(c) Superprime

Figure 5.10. Macroeconomic fits of the roll to default showing the in-sample fit and extrapolation under the three DFAST economic scenarios: base, adverse, and severe.

5.3 State-level Models

In comparison to the national model, the state levels provide a view into the diversity of possible answers. Figures 5.11 – 5.13 provide examples for the rolls to buckets 1, 3, and 5 representing early, mid, and late delinquency. The payment rate economic model is not shown, because the results are the same as for the time series model in Figure 4.9.

The economic model for roll to bucket 1, Figure 5.11 had the most diversity in macroeconomic factors of the roll rates and the most economic dependency overall. From the figure, HPI was the most important factor overall, with the least dependency for superprime and the most for subprime and prime. However, in Figure 5.12, HPI was again most important, but this time with the dependencies reversed—most important for superprime and least important for subprime.

Unemployment rate appears in the model for roll to bucket 1 with three different transformations: difference, log-ratio, and moving average. Of these, log-ratio is the most important, particularly for superprime. Disposable personal income (DPI) and GDP show as equally important overall, but with dependencies by segment exactly reversed—subprime being most sensitive to DPI and superprime being most sensitive to GDP.

The roll to bucket 3 economic dependencies, Figure 5.12, for GDP and unemployment are reversed as compared to roll 1, just as HPI was. Only DPI keeps the same ranking across segments for both roll 1 and roll 3.

The roll to bucket 5 is simpler than the previous rolls, with only four factors showing any significance and HPI appearing to be the only important one. At this stage, the three risk grades have nearly equal use of HPI.

5.4 Forecasting

For forecasting, scenarios are applied to each of the roll rate models above to roll the outstanding balances to either of the two terminal states, pay-off or default. Charge-offs that could occur outside the roll rate structure, such as bankruptcy, fraud, or deceased charge-offs are treated as if they had actually rolled, so roll to charge-off can exceed 100%.

Figure 5.14 shows an example of how balances roll through the delinquency states. The top table shows historical actuals for both bal-

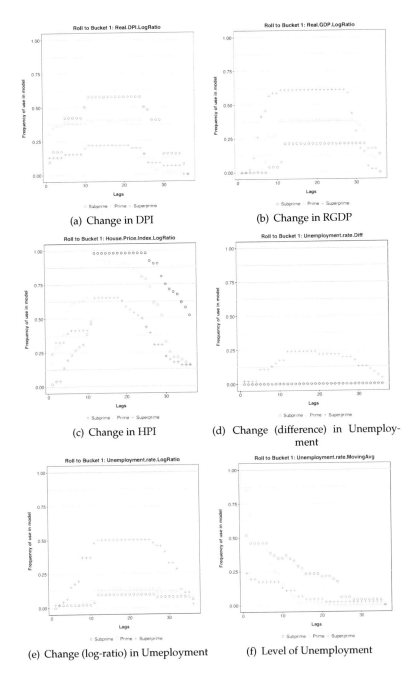

Figure 5.11. Macroeconomic dependencies for roll to bucket 1 averaged across all state-level and risk grade models.

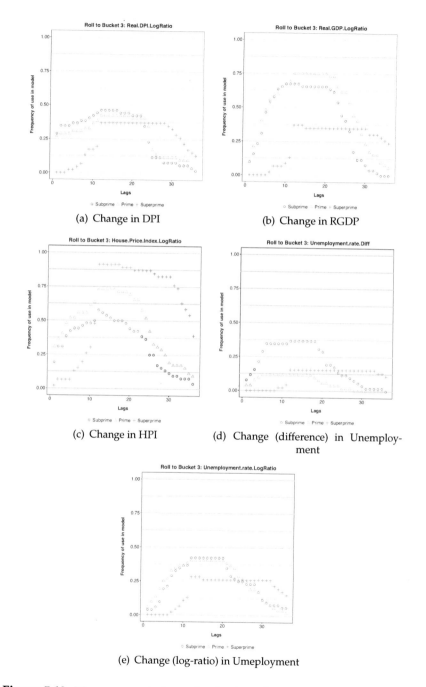

(a) Change in DPI

(b) Change in RGDP

(c) Change in HPI

(d) Change (difference) in Unemployment

(e) Change (log-ratio) in Umeployment

Figure 5.12. Macroeconomic dependencies for roll to bucket 3 averaged across all state-level and risk grade models.

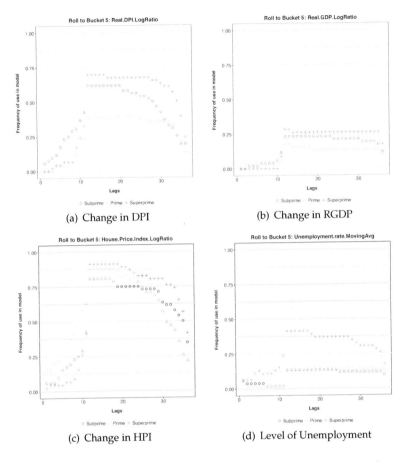

(a) Change in DPI

(b) Change in RGDP

(c) Change in HPI

(d) Level of Unemployment

Figure 5.13. Macroeconomic dependencies for roll to bucket 5 averaged across all state-level and risk grade models.

ances (in millions $) and the corresponding roll rates. The forecasts in the lower panel are created using an average of the roll rates for the previous six months. The blue shaded cells contain the six-month average roll rates. The green shaded cells show the forecasted balances resulting from those roll rates.

Although called a "moving average", the roll rates for February 2007 should not include the average roll rates estimated for January 2007. Although sometimes done, such moving averages to no include any additional information and serve only to add noise.

In a typical roll rate structure structure, new originations would be required in order to estimate future Current balances. Without such information, the lower roll rate panel only shows projections from the last

1,000,000s	Jun-06	Jul-06		Aug-06		Sep-06		Oct-06		Nov-06		Dec-06	
Current	1,223,180	1,247,766		1,265,587		1,280,602		1,288,530		1,300,809		1,316,352	
30-59 DPD	14,789	15,412	1.3%	15,888	1.3%	17,266	1.4%	17,561	1.4%	17,996	1.4%	19,760	1.5%
60-89 DPD	2,827	2,976	20.1%	3,090	20.0%	3,335	21.0%	3,473	20.1%	3,528	20.1%	3,772	21.0%
90-119 DPD	1,049	1,105	39.1%	1,137	38.2%	1,194	38.7%	1,253	37.6%	1,291	37.2%	1,354	38.4%
120-149 DPD	607	613	58.4%	647	58.5%	666	58.6%	724	60.6%	767	61.2%	798	61.8%
150-179 DPD	372	383	63.1%	400	65.3%	422	65.2%	453	68.0%	497	68.7%	524	68.3%
Charge-off	251	233	62.5%	237	61.9%	265	66.3%	273	64.8%	297	65.5%	336	67.7%

1,000,000s	Jan-07		Feb-07		Mar-07		Apr-07		May-07		Jun-07	
Current												
30-59 DPD	17,956	1.4%										
60-89 DPD	4,029	20.4%	3,661	20.4%								
90-119 DPD	1,440	38.2%	1,538	38.2%	1,398	38.2%						
120-149 DPD	810	59.9%	862	59.9%	921	59.9%	837	59.9%				
150-179 DPD	530	66.4%	538	66.4%	573	66.4%	612	66.4%	556	66.4%		
Charge-off	340	64.8%	343	64.8%	349	64.8%	371	64.8%	396	64.8%	360	64.8%

Figure 5.14. Table showing historic roll rate data and a forecast using 6-month averages of the roll rates.

known current balance. This leads to the perception that roll rates are good for the first six months of a forecast, because those estimates can be created largely without any assumptions on future originations. In a CECL context, no new originations are be included, and a pay-down rate is used to reduce the current balance to zero through the lifetime forecast.

A moving average roll rate model is quite common, but it does not incorporate macroeconomic factors. For the CECL estimation, the roll rate models estimated above are used instead of the six month moving averages.

5.5 Possible Enhancements

One of the weaknesses with roll rates is the noise in the later rolls. For less massive datasets, rolls for buckets 3 through 5 tend to look like mostly noise. In such cases, a simple moving average may be more accurate than trying to create actual models. This may also improve the small sample size performance observed for the roll rate models shown in Section 2.1.3.

As mentioned before, roll rates are not really a model, but a system of equations. As such, they could be modeled any number of ways. One common approach is to apply vintage modeling to the roll rates. Each roll rate time series can be split by vintage so that lifecycle and credit quality effects may be included in the roll rate forecasts. This has been observed to be significantly more accurate than the time series models of roll rates shown here. Of course, it is also significantly more work. The term "roll rates" rarely refers to "vintage rate modeling, but many such hybrids are possible.

6

Vintage Models

Rather than model a single time series of performance through time, vintage models aggregate the data by origination cohort (vintage). The set of vintage time series is modeled collectively in order to capture the expected dynamics versus age of the loan, credit quality with vintage, and performance with calendar date.

Vintage analysis in the context of creating vintage graphs versus age of the loan or calendar date have been around for many decades. Figure 6.1 shows an annual vintage graph by age of the account, also known as months-on-books. A graph like this can be read to compare performance between vintages to get an intuitive perspective on vintage credit quality. The graph clearly shows that the 2006, 2007, and 2008 vintages are different from the rest even in the first couple of years. The 2009 vintage is dramatically improved, and the subsequent vintages are better yet. The graph of vintage performance by calendar date shown in Figure 6.2 also provides intuition on the causes of the peaks in the 2005-2008 vintages. Note that both graphs show the same data, just aligned differently. The monthly vintages were aligned before aggregation when creating the graph by age.

Modern vintage analysis is simply using mathematical means to quantify what can already be seen in a vintage graph. This model uses the Age-Period-Cohort (APC) algorithm to decompose segmented data, followed by econometric modeling of the APC environment function, linking it to macroeconomic variables. The first known vintage analysis was in the form of the Lexis diagram used in demography (Goldman 1992, Keiding 1990, Keyfitz 1968, Lexis 1875, Vandenschrick 2001). However, the mathematical foundations of APC algorithms were established in the 1960s (Glenn 2005, Mason and Fienberg 1985, Ryder 1965). Simpler methods of vintage analysis are available, but APC models have the most robust literature and are well established in retail lending (Breeden and Thomas 2008, Breeden et al. 2008). Breeden (Breeden 2014) provides an extensive treatment of the use of vintage models in retail lending.

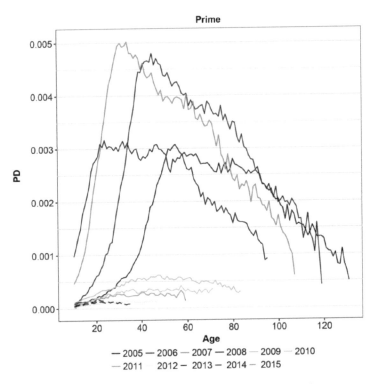

Figure 6.1. A graph of annual vintages aligned by age of the account, also known as months-on-books.

The following key steps are used in creating the models:

1. Run APC-style decomposition on the key variables to produce:
    (a) Lifecycle function by loan age
    (b) Vintage quality function by vintage
    (c) Environment function by calendar date
    (d) Seasonality function by month of the year

2. Create macroeconomic models to predict the environment functions for the key rates using optimally transformed macroeconomic factors.

3. Create forecasts of the environment function by applying the macroeconomic model to the mean-reverting scenarios.

4. Combine the environment function extrapolations with previous estimates of lifecycle, vintage quality, and seasonality to create forecasts.

The vintage models follow a modified Basel II approach, modeling default rate, aka probability of default (PD), exposure at default (EAD), and probability of attrition (PA). PA is not included in the Basel II equations, but is necessary for lifetime loss projection. Loss given default (LGD) is not modeled here, because it is assumed to be a constant as with all the other models. Equations 6.1 – 6.3 give the mathematical definitions of these rates.

$$PD(t) = \frac{\text{Default accounts}(t)}{\text{Active accounts}(t-1)} \tag{6.1}$$

$$EAD(t) = \frac{\text{Default balance}(t)}{\text{Default accounts}(t)} \tag{6.2}$$

$$PA(t) = \frac{\text{Attrition accounts}(t)}{\text{Active accounts}(t-1)} \tag{6.3}$$

Each of the above key rates is created from the historical data and decomposed using APC to quantify the lifecycle versus age of the loan, environment function versus calendar date, vintage function by origination date (vintage), and seasonality where appropriate. Separate functions are created by risk grade and additionally by state for the state-level models.

6.1 APC Decomposition

The basic concept for APC is similar to survival and hazard models. In all these methods, the age of the account is a key determinant of performance. This is referred to as the lifecycle, hazard function, or loss timing function in the case of loss forecasting. The lifecycle function will exhibit different shapes by key rate and product. In graphs, the lifecycle function is usually transformed back to the units of the key rate to aid intuition.

APC models differ from survival and hazard models in that the latter are loan-level models, whereas APC models analyze vintage-aggregate performance data. Survival models are explored separately as a candidate technique for CECL.

In addition to the lifecycle versus age of the loan, the APC algorithm quantifies as a vintage function measured relative to that lifecycle. A

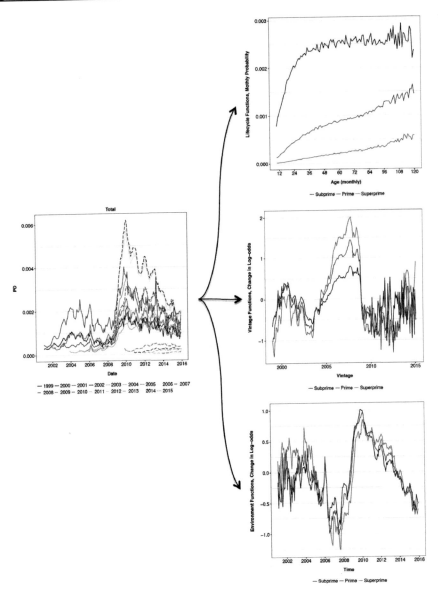

Figure 6.2. A Visualization of the decomposition of the default rate vintage data. The analysis was split by risk grade segments.

value of zero for the function indicates that a vintage is exactly like the lifecycle—average risk. When predicting default probability, the values of the vintage quality function measure incremental risk in units of log-odds, much like a FICO score is linear in log-odds.

The vintage function is measured just from the performance data, so new vintages will have significantly higher uncertainty than older vintages. When modeling default rate, the most recent six months of vintages will have almost no data to model and thus will be very rough approximations. Older vintages are well quantified.

The environment function is measured relative to the lifecycle on a specific calendar date, where the zero level is set to the lifecycle. Changes in the environment function indicate how much incremental risk in units of log-odds occurs on a specific calendar date. Due to seasonality or macroeconomic influences, periods occur where all vintages exhibit higher-than-average losses when compared to their lifecycle estimates. This effect is quantified in the environment function.

If seasonality is determined to be important, it may be extracted from the environment function, since both are calendar time-based.

Figure 6.2 illustrates how vintage-aggregate performance data for default rate was decomposed into these primary functions, split by risk grade segments. The optional seasonality component was not estimated here.

1. Lifecycle, $F(a)$: The top graph on the right quantifies the expected rate as a function of the age of the loan (months-on-book). The y-axis is scaled to the observed rate, in this case the monthly default rate. Three lines are shown for subprime, prime, and superprime from highest rate to lowest rate. Subprime peaks fastest and superprime never does.

2. Vintage quality, $G(v)$: The middle graph on the right provides a measure of net credit quality by vintage, normalizing for lifecycle and environment. The y-axis is measured in terms of the change in log-odds where the zero level is the lifecycle function. This example illustrates a period of high-risk loan origination in 2006-2008, followed by a much lower risk loan origination period from 2009 to present. The superprime segment is the most dynamic through the credit cycle with twice as much variation as subprime.

3. Environment, $H(t)$: The bottom graph on the right provides a measure of the net impact as a function of calendar date. The y-axis is scaled as the change in log-odds as measured relative to the lifecycle. For small changes, the difference between two points on the graph is roughly the percentage change in rate. In this example, the recession in 2009 shows a peak in the default rate and 2011-2015 show steady declines in default rates. Note that all three risk grades show the same relative impacts from the envir-

onment. Because of this, the environment functions are combined for later analysis while the lifecycle and vintage functions are kept separate by risk grade.

Mathematically, this approach expresses each rate as being decomposed according to Equation 6.4 with $Ssn(s)$ representing seasonality.

$$r(a = t - v, v, t, s = t \bmod 12) =$$
$$\text{Link}(F(a) + G(v) + H(t) + Ssn(s)) \tag{6.4}$$

The *Link* function depends upon the distribution of the variable being analyzed. Default and attrition have binomial distributions, so a logit link function is used, $\text{logit}(x) = \log(x/(1-x))$.

Balance rates like EAD are usually log-normally distributed, so a logarithm is applied to the balance ratios prior to APC-style modeling with a Normal distribution.

The incorporation of macroeconomic effects in the vintage analysis follows the method of Breeden, et. al. (Breeden and Thomas 2008). The macroeconomic modeling is performed separately from the initial decomposition so as not to introduce colinearity problems between macroeconomic factors and the lifecycle or vintage functions. Once the environment function is extracted from the vintage data, the goal is to compare the environment function to lagged values of transformed independent macroeconomic factors.

6.2 Specification errors

Vintage analysis highlights a problem in analyzing retail loan portfolios, $a = t - v$. The age of the loan is equal to the calendar date minus the vintage date. Because of this simple expression, when functions of age, vintage, and time are estimated, a linear specification error will occur unless corrections are made. Holford explains well that a decision must be made about the trend ambiguity in any vintage analysis, whereby only two linear components can be estimated from the three available dimensions. This decision is always domain-specific. The assumption that a through-the-cycle probability-of-default can be defined as in Basel II and other banking regulations is equivalent in the present context to assuming that the environment function has no net trend if measured over a full economic cycle. Therefore, we build that assumption into our estimation equation as a solution to the trend specification problem and later test the robustness of this assumption by reviewing backward and forward extrapolations of the environment function with macroeconomic data to show that no net trend has been introduced.

The following form, Equation 6.5, is used for estimating the APC components:

$$p(a, v, t) \sim c_0 + c_1 a + F'(a) + c_2 v + G'(v) + H'(t) \qquad (6.5)$$

$F'(a)$, $G'(v)$, and $H'(t)$ are the nonlinear components of lifecycle, vintage quality, and environment, respectively. The final functions produced from the decomposition are

$$F(a) = c_0 + c_1 a + F'(a) \qquad (6.6)$$
$$G(v) = c_2 v + G'(v) \qquad (6.7)$$
$$H(t) = H'(t) \qquad (6.8)$$

Note that the constant term is added to the lifecycle just as a matter of convention, so that the lifecycle is scaled to the original data. Holford (Holford 1983) also provides a proof that the components of the estimation equation shown above can be uniquely determined from vintage data.

The discussion here of a linear specification problem in APC estimation is a comment about the data, not the APC algorithm. The non-parametric approach in APC simply exposes the problem explicitly. If one of the three nonparametric functions was replaced with explanatory factors, as happens in Cox proportional hazards models or any factor-based regression model, the linear specification problem is transformed into a multicolinearity problem. No modeling algorithm for retail loans is immune from this problem. They simply express it in different ways.

Also note that because the nonlinear components are uniquely estimable, as long as more than one full economic cycle is present in the data, all the important structure will be captured and the specification problem naturally disappears.

Typical implementations of APC algorithms use spline interpolation to estimate these three functions, which implies that the functions are continuous, at least theoretically. Although the lifecycles in Figure 6.2 may be continuous with perfect data, the vintage and environment functions are theoretically discontinuous because sudden shocks may occur in either. Therefore, a quick spline estimation of these functions was used only as a prior for the more detailed Bayesian estimation shown in Figure 6.2.

6.3 Bayesian APC

Bayesian APC estimates each point of the lifecycle, environment, and vintage functions without the smoothness constraint of the APC spline estimation. It uses the spline functions as an initial prior, but then uses a Monte Carlo estimation procedure to refine the functions. The result looks "noisier", but it has the ability to better estimate the complex structure that can arise in the functions. For example, the bankruptcy law spike is clearly visible in the environment function and completely cleaned from the lifecycle and vintage functions. Similarly, the vintage function may have apparent discontinuities because of sudden changes in underwriting policies.

The Bayesian APC implementation followed the work by Schmid and Held (Schmid and Held 2007). The essential parameters in the Bayesian APC control the number of Monte Carlo simulations used to create the estimate and the step size for each simulation. These values were set high enough that the functions and their error bars converged.

6.4 Decomposition Results

The decomposition results for probability of default were shown in Figure 6.2. In this section the same analysis is shown for probability of attrition and exposure at default.

Figure 6.3 shows the Bayesian APC decomposition for the probability of default. The lifecycle function by risk grade shows that for all consumers, no one wants to refinance their mortgage within a year of taking out the loan. For subprime, the peak attrition period is at about 24 months. Prime mortgages have a constant risk of attrition (assumed to be mostly refinance) between 24 and 72 months. Superprime loans don't reach a saturation level until 36 months, meaning they are even more reluctant to refinance early in the life of a loan. These are all 30 year fixed-rate mortgages, so none of this structure relates to teaser rate or adjustable rate periods. Issues such as those have been studied before and would appear more dramatically in these curves (Trudolyubov and Breeden 2011).

Some of the structure in the probability of attrition lifecycle function is probably related to the frequency with which Americans move to a new home. Data from the US Census Bureau indicate that the average American will move around 11.3 to 11.7 times in their lifetime. Given an average lifespan of about 79 years, that would mean moving about every

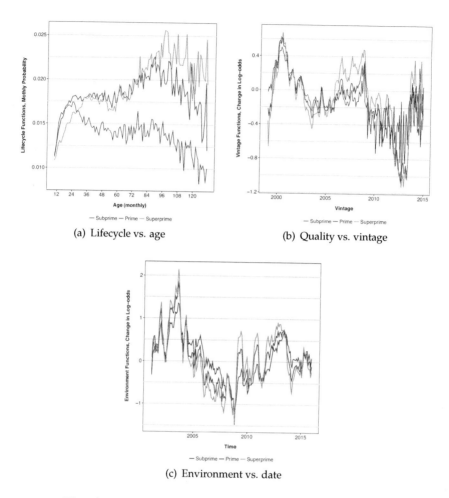

(a) Lifecycle vs. age

(b) Quality vs. vintage

(c) Environment vs. date

Figure 6.3. Decomposition results for probability of attrition.

6.9 years. The time to 50% probability of attrition for a loan is around 5 years, which can be obtained by making the probability of attrition lifecycle graph into a cumulative (survival) function. This would appear to be a reasonable result considering the propensity for Americans to move and the typical historical refinance opportunities.

The vintage function, Figure 6.3(b), shows the risk of each vintage attriting, most likely from a refinance. The structure here should be correlated mostly to the initial interest rate of the loan. Higher interest rate loans are more likely to refinance at some future point.

The environment function captures periods of attrition that may be higher or lower, possibly due to changes in interest rates or economic

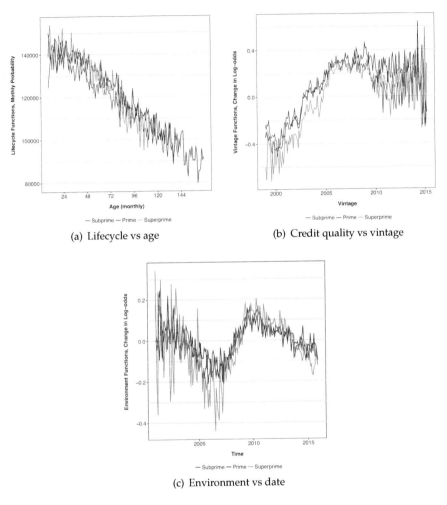

(a) Lifecycle vs age

(b) Credit quality vs vintage

(c) Environment vs date

Figure 6.4. Decomposition results for exposure at default fraction.

conditions for the borrowers. Those details are captured in the next part of the analysis.

Figure 6.4 shows the decomposition of exposure at default. EAD does not include any recoveries or asset values. This is purely the dynamics of the outstanding balance at time of default.

The lifecycle function, Figure 6.4(a), has a bit of estimation noise, but clearly just follows the balance pay-down with account age. In a loan-level model, once could compute the expected payments, and that will be shown later. In an aggregate model, the data has a blend of interest rates and balances, so the lifecycle here just models the average pay-down for an average loan.

Default balance could also be modeled as an exposure at default fraction, or $EADf(a) = EAD(a)/$Initial Loan Amount(0). this should be bounded between 0 and 1 and in some portfolios might be estimated more robustly.

The vintage function, Figure 6.4(b) mostly calibrates the lifecycle to the different initial loan amounts by vintage. Clearly the loan amounts were higher just prior to the recession and then came down as loan origination became more conservative. If the vintages trended higher through the data, that would suggest than an EADf approach might be most stable.

Lastly the environment function, Figure 6.4(c), shows some variation with default balances, appearing to roughly track the economic cycle. The variation here is much less than is seen for the probabilities of default and attrition, since most consumers either make the scheduled payment. Clearly prepayment via attrition (complete loan pay-off) is the dominant form of balance pay-down.

6.5 Macroeconomic Models

Macroeconomic models were created for the various environment functions so as to predict the future environment given a macroeconomic scenario. The approach was the same as in Chapter 4, except that the target variable was only the environment component from the decomposition of a key rate rather than the entire rate. This way, the economic modeling does not also try to explain changes in origination volume or underwriting.

Figures 6.5 – 6.7 show the best in-sample fits to the PD, PA, and EADf environment functions.

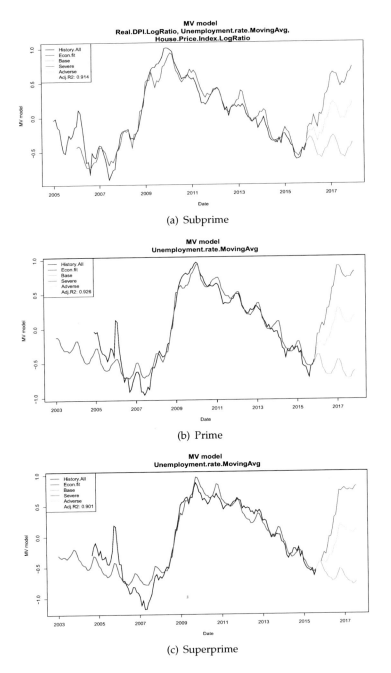

Figure 6.5. Macroeconomic fits of the environment function for probability of default showing the in-sample fit and extrapolation under the three DFAST economic scenarios: base, adverse, and severe.

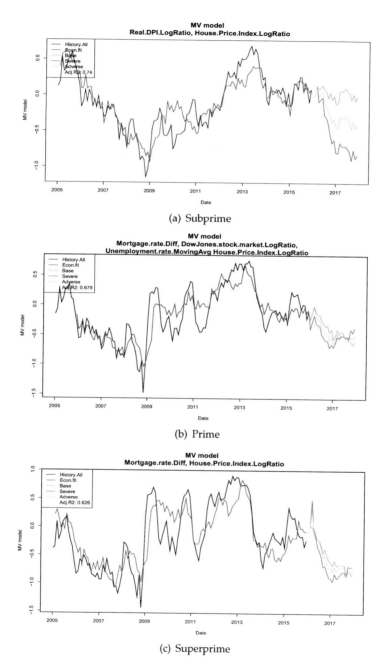

Figure 6.6. Macroeconomic fits of the environment function for probability of attrition showing the in-sample fit and extrapolation under the three DFAST economic scenarios: base, adverse, and severe.

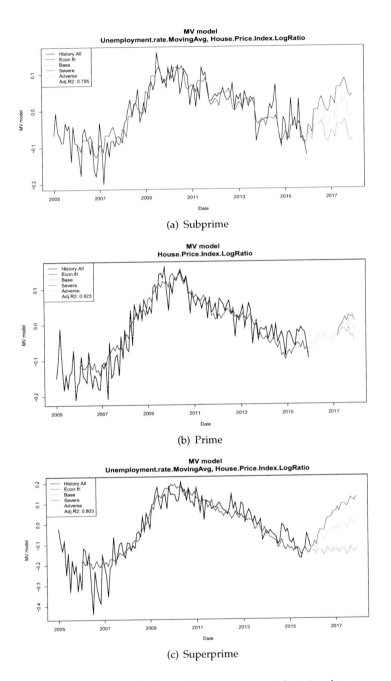

(a) Subprime

(b) Prime

(c) Superprime

Figure 6.7. Macroeconomic fits of the environment function for exposure at default showing the in-sample fit and extrapolation under the three DFAST economic scenarios: base, adverse, and severe.

6.6 Structural Tests

All models assume that the structures learned historically will persist into the forecast period. The effectiveness of a model is the extent to which this is true. Although one can test models by re-estimating coefficients on different segment of the data, multicolinearity often makes such tests meaningless. Colinear factors may be assigned different coefficients from different time spans yet produce the same composite forecast.

A more useful test is to compare separable parts of the models. Determining what is separable, or uniquely estimable can be challenging, but the literature on APC models proves that lifecycle, vintage, and environment are separable except for a linear trend. Therefore, tests can be designed to see if the structures trained in-sample are robust to other segments of the data.

6.6.1 Alternating vintage test

Similar to the way score cards are tested on randomly selected sets of in-sample and out-of-sample accounts, vintage models can be tested by splitting the vintages into two segments. With enough vintages, a random selection could be used, but a simple alternating segmentation can be used: Odds (Jan, Mar, May, Jul, Sep, Nov) and Evens (Feb, Apr, Jun, Aug, Oct, Dec). If these completely independent segments produce the same lifecycle and environment, then the basic theory of APC models is more justified.

Figures 6.8 – 6.11 show the test results for the PD and PA models. Visually, the lifecycle and environment functions for both rates are right on top of each other. This is a philosophically comforting result. Two completely separate datasets with no overlapping accounts produce exactly the same results. Even though the algorithm produces confidence intervals, this is a strong statement about the presence of the structures being measured.

To perform a statistical test with p-values, the point-by-point distance can be measured between the nonlinear components of the two functions, normalized by the confidence intervals.

$$\chi^2 = \sum_i \frac{(y_1(i) - y_2(i))^2}{\sigma_1^2(i) + \sigma_2^2(i)} \tag{6.9}$$

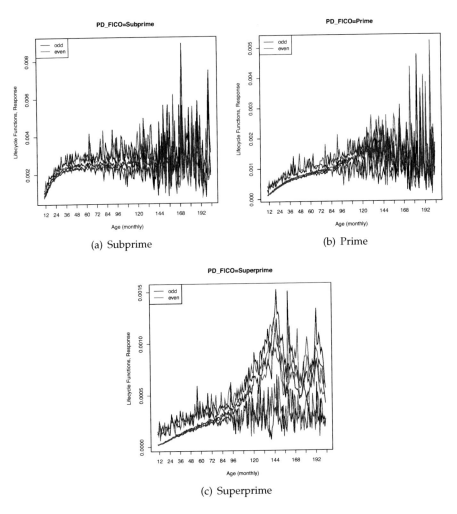

(a) Subprime   (b) Prime

(c) Superprime

Figure 6.8. Results of alternating vintage test for PD lifecycle functions.

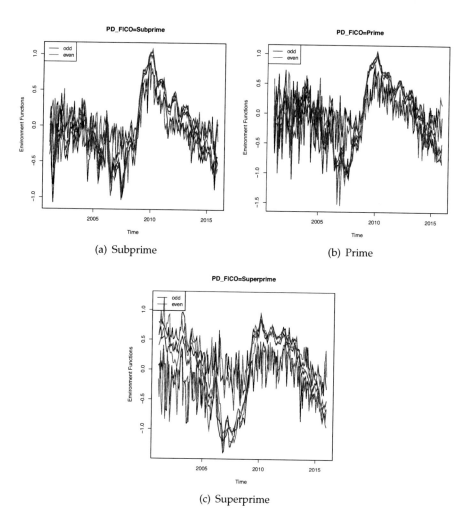

(a) Subprime

(b) Prime

(c) Superprime

Figure 6.9. Results of alternating vintage test for PD environment functions.

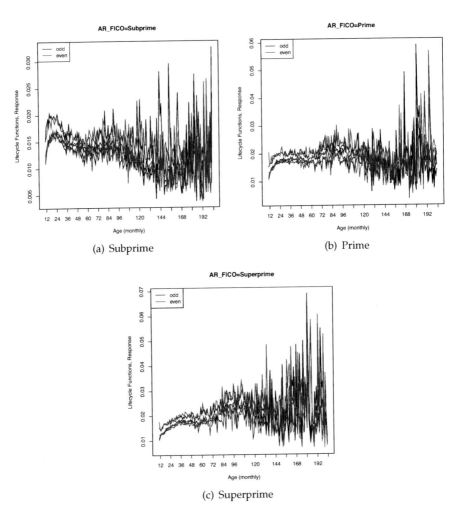

(a) Subprime

(b) Prime

(c) Superprime

Figure 6.10. Results of alternating vintage test for PA lifecycle functions.

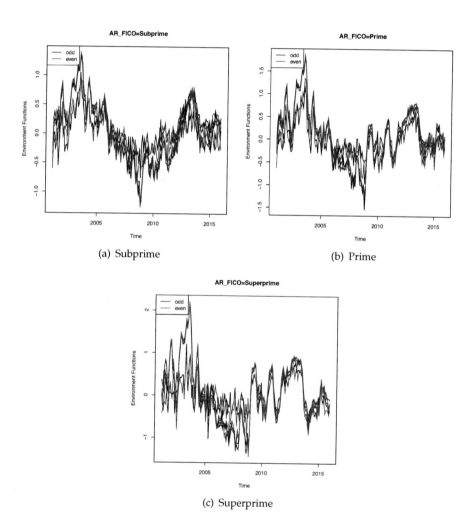

(a) Subprime

(b) Prime

(c) Superprime

Figure 6.11. Results of alternating vintage test for PA environment functions.

where $y_1(i)$ and $y_2(i)$ are the series being tested and $\sigma_1(i)$ and $\sigma_2(i)$ are the corresponding confidence intervals, all measured at point i along the functions. The measure would follow a χ^2 distribution.

Table 6.1 shows the test results. A value near 1.0 indicates confidence that the estimates are not different. From this, all of the functions are very confidently the same, as is obvious visually.

Function	Variable	Segment	χ^2	Df	p-value
Age	PA	Subprime	18.59	122	1
Age	PA	Prime	32.81	122	1
Age	PA	Superprime	24.72	122	1
Age	PD	Subprime	19.44	117	1
Age	PD	Prime	6.43	117	1
Age	PD	Superprime	3.67	117	1
Time	PA	Subprime	25.05	179	1
Time	PA	Prime	24.39	179	1
Time	PA	Superprime	32.25	179	1
Time	PD	Subprime	35.78	179	1
Time	PD	Prime	43.08	179	1
Time	PD	Superprime	14.48	179	1

Table 6.1. Results of the χ^2 test for the alternating vintage test.

6.6.2 Old vintage / new vintage test

For APC models, the alternating vintage test almost never fails. The key dimensions of an APC model are robustly observable, so long as the same time span is covered.

A much more rigorous test is the old vintage / new vintage test, testing the assumption that the lifecycle does not change through time. Whenever someone says, "We don't include the older data in our models because our originations were much different then", respond with, "There's a test for that." If the product is largely unchanged and the segmentation is stable, the test should pass. Conversely, if the test fails, the solution is usually to segment the data along the dimension of the portfolio or product changes.

Figures 6.12 – 6.15 show the functions obtained from the old and new vintages when splitting on 2009. The lifecycle functions appear to be different, but they include constant and linear terms by convention.

A better approach for assessing the segmentation is to test only the nonlinear parts. Figures 6.16 – 6.17 compare the nonlinear parts of the

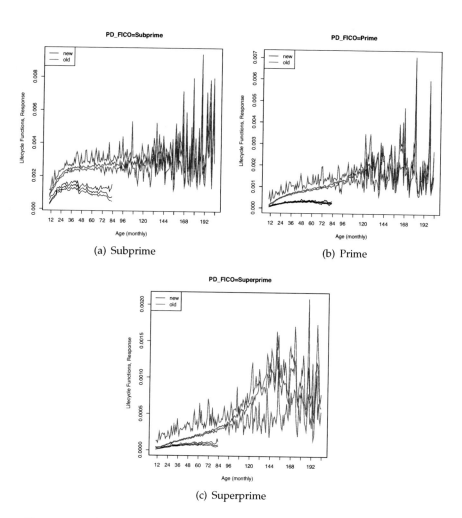

Figure 6.12. Results of old vintage / new vintage test for PD lifecycle functions.

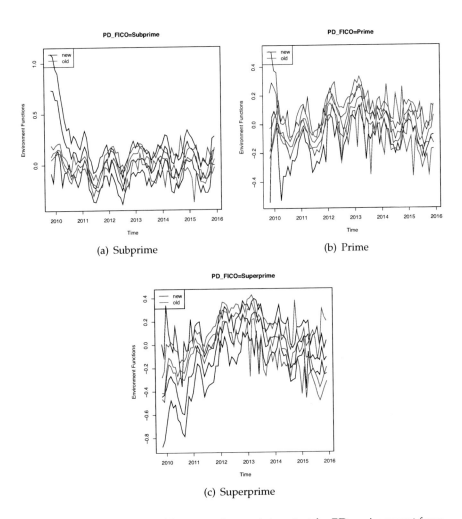

Figure 6.13. Results of old vintage / new vintage test for PD environment functions.

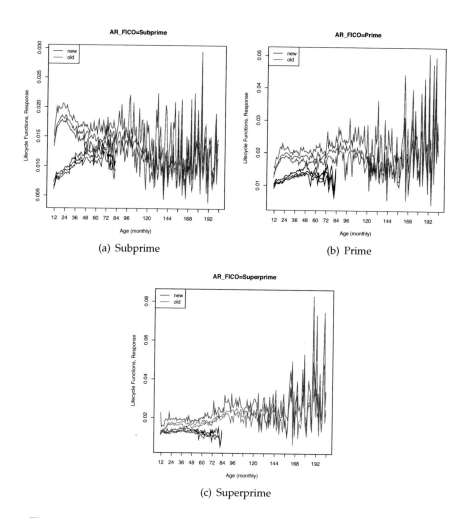

(a) Subprime

(b) Prime

(c) Superprime

Figure 6.14. Results of old vintage / new vintage test for PA lifecycle functions.

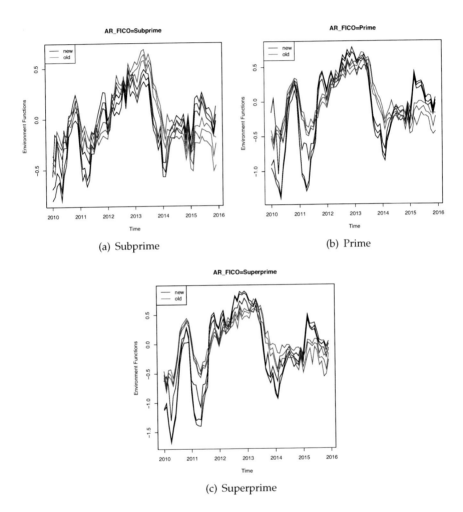

(a) Subprime

(b) Prime

(c) Superprime

Figure 6.15. Results of old vintage / new vintage test for PA environment functions.

lifecycles. Note that, by assumption, the envirnoemnt functions do not include constant or linear terms, so those are already being compared correctly.

Performing the χ^2 test produces the results in Table 6.2. Those results confirm what can be seen in the figures. The environment functions are the same in some cases and similar but not exactly the same in others. Although some of the differences are not large, the test is sensitive to such divergences. The issue seems to be that the new vintages follow the same pattern as the old vintages, but with a more dynamic range for PA.

For the age functions, after removing the constant and linear terms, the PD lifecycles are surprisingly similar. The χ^2 test again confirms what is visually obvious. For the PA lifecycles, there do appear to be some structural differences that exceed the confidence intervals. The older vintages have a greater chance of pay-off in the first 24 months than the newer vintages.

Function	Variable	Segment	χ^2	Df	p-value
Age	PA	Subprime	78.09	73	0.32
Age	PA	Prime	70.83	73	0.55
Age	PA	Superprime	85.48	73	0.15
Age	PD	Subprime	22.46	74	1.00
Age	PD	Prime	15.11	74	1.00
Age	PD	Superprime	7.55	74	1.00
Time	PA	Subprime	103.68	72	0.01
Time	PA	Prime	273.88	72	0.00
Time	PA	Superprime	334.50	72	0.00
Time	PD	Subprime	23.46	74	1.00
Time	PD	Prime	15.24	74	1.00
Time	PD	Superprime	9.64	74	1.00

Table 6.2. Results of the χ^2 test for the old vintage / new vintage test.

This suggests that the new vintages for PA are different in ways bey-ond risk segmentation. Although the accuracy tests show that the model works well overall, the PA modeling could be improved with additional segmentation to bring these functions into alignment.

The alternating vintage test and old vintage / new vintage test are obvious ways to test the stability of a vintage model. However, they could be performed on any model described here. To save space and time, these tests are not replicated for all models, but a roll rate or state

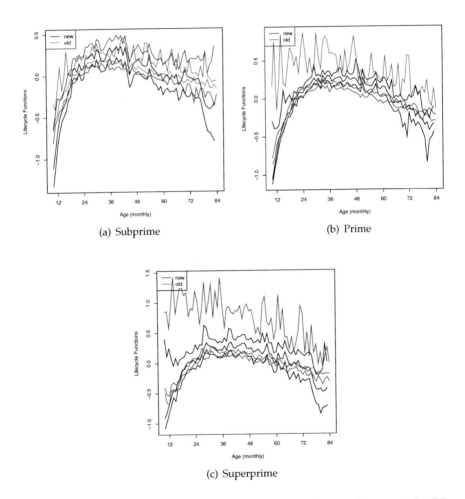

(a) Subprime

(b) Prime

(c) Superprime

Figure 6.16. Nonlinear components of old vintage / new vintage test for PD lifecycle functions.

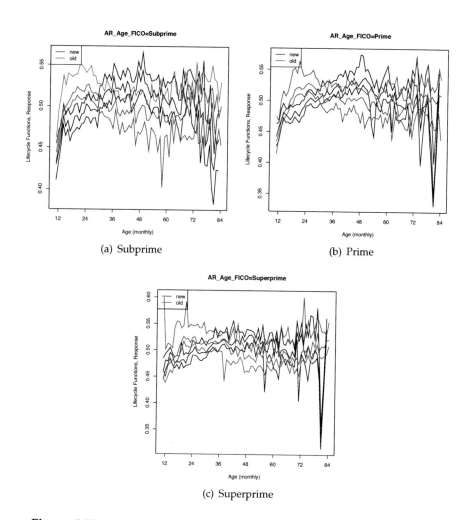

Figure 6.17. Nonlinear components of old vintage / new vintage test for PA lifecycle functions.

transition model could be tested by vintage. The fact that vintage is not an explicit component of the model is irrelevant to the test.

6.7 State-level Models

When testing vintage modeling on 52 US states and provinces, the entire process was repeated independently for each segment. Independent decompositions were estimated for each segment and the environment functions were modeled with macroeconomic factors.

As a simple summary of all these models, Figures 6.18 – 6.20 show the frequency of use of various lag values for the macroeconomic factors.

6.8 Forecasting

Vintage models forecasts are created, obviously, at the vintage level. Although a single equation, Equation 6.4 creates the forecast in a single step, the forecasts can be visualized as a process of refinement. Figure 6.21 shows an example of forecasting the prime November 2015 vintage. With no other information than "prime segment" for the mortgage data in the study, the black line would be the forecast—the average environment, average credit quality forecast.

However, the November 2005 vintage comes from a period of increasingly risky loan originations. Within six months of origination, the true credit quality begins to be measured. From those early measurements, the red line would be the revised forecast. Late 2005 was actually a better than average economic environment, such that the credit risk and environment were cancelling and thus returning the forecast back to the lifecycle average. Using actual economic conditions, the forecast for months 24 through 60 show that when the environment returns to average and then falls into recession, the forecasted vintage performance deteriorates rapidly.

The final line in the graph shows the inclusion of seasonality. Since it is estimated as mean-zero through the year, this only adds some variation about the previous line.

The author was actually creating vintage models for mortgage portfolios in early 2006 that predicted the red line under a flattening economy scenario. If economic conditions just stopped improving, performance would relax onto the curve representing the intrinsic credit quality of the vintages. Even before a recession began, losses started

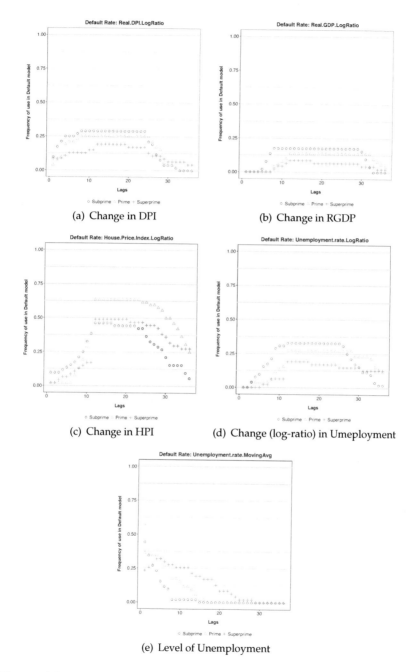

Figure 6.18. Macroeconomic dependencies of the environment function for probability of default in the vintage model, averaged across all state-level and risk grade models.

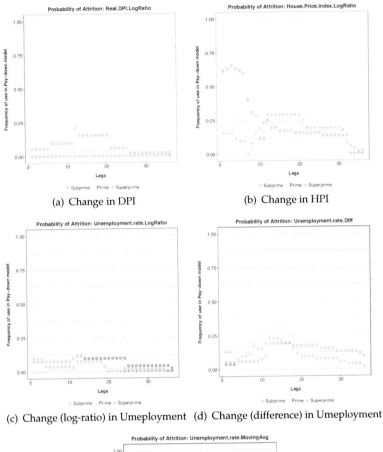

(a) Change in DPI   (b) Change in HPI

(c) Change (log-ratio) in Umeployment   (d) Change (difference) in Umeployment

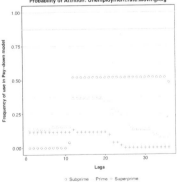

(e) Level of Unemployment

Figure 6.19. Macroeconomic dependencies of the environment function for probability of attrition in the vintage model, averaged across all state-level and risk grade models.

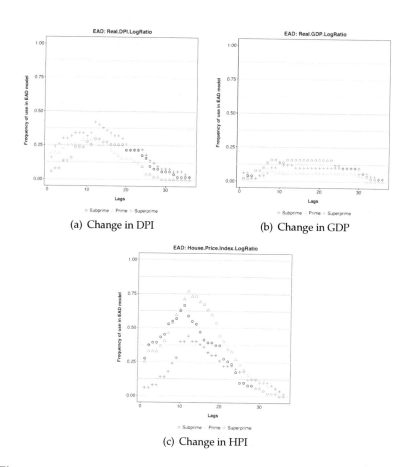

(a) Change in DPI

(b) Change in GDP

(c) Change in HPI

Figure 6.20. Macroeconomic dependencies of the environment function for exposure at default in the vintage model, averaged across all state-level and risk grade models.

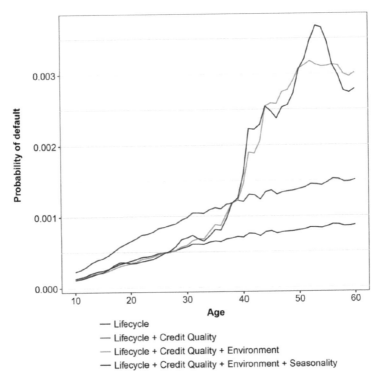

Figure 6.21. A visual example of how the components of a vintage model are combined to create a final vintage forecast. This example is for the Prime mortgage vintage from November 2005.

to mount because of the combination of risky vintages and a flattening economy.

6.9 Possible Enhancements

Vintage models have three components (age, vintage, and time) that are independent except for linear trends. With enough data, as in this study, this means that the model develop has quite a bit of flexibility in combining functions across segments. For example, the 52 independent US state and province models did not need to be fully independent. The product lifecycles for PD and EAD are logically similar across all states and need only to be segmented by risk grade. Economic modeling could be separate by state, but seasonality estimates may be regional largely due to the weather.

Modularity in vintage models also provides some unique flexibility. For a portfolio without enough history for an APC decomposition, a lifecycle could be borrowed from another analysis and used to see the decomposition. Similarly, a time series of industry-wide performance might be transformed to serve as a proxy for the environment function to seed the analysis. Such flexibility makes vintage models particularly useful in limited data situations.

For the probability of attrition modeling, after the initial decomposition, the vintage and environment functions could possibly be replaced with a measure of change in interest rate since the loan originated and some additional economic factors such as HPI and unemployment. If this were a loan-level model, looking at change in property value for the borrower's home would also be interesting. However, for an aggregate model, such loan-level details wash out. HPI is sufficient to capture such trends.

7

State Transition Models

State transition models are the loan-level equivalent of roll rate models. They derive from Markov models, though in practice they may not satisfy the Markov criteria that no history other than the current state is used in the model. They were used first and most heavily for corporate ratings and commercial lending, where most of the literature is still to be found (Israel et al. 2000, Truck 2014, Wei 2003). However, they are also well-used for retail lending, most often for mortgages (Bangia et al. 2002, Thomas et al. 2001). The method used here is most like that of Berteloot, et. al. (Berteloot et al. 2013).

Rather than modeling aggregate movements between delinquency states as in roll rate models, the probability of transition is computed for each account. The states considered here are current, delinquent up to a maximum of five months, default, and attrition (complete pay-off), Figure 7.1. In this model, account transition probabilities are predicted rather than the dollar transitions in the roll rate model.

If a portfolio was managed such that default is declared at six months delinquent, then the total number of active states would be six (current plus five delinquency states). If a loan in any active state can transition to any other active state, default, or attrition, then the total number of transitions is $(n+1)^2 + 2(n+1)$ for n delinquency states and including the transitions to default or payoff. This gives a total of 48 transitions for $n = 5$.

If balances were modeled instead of accounts, the transition probabilities for each state would not add to 1, because balances may grow or shrink through the transitions. That uncertainty would add to the number of transitions that must be modeled, with the result that modeling balances requires the same number of variables as modeling account transition probabilities and then balance per account in each state.

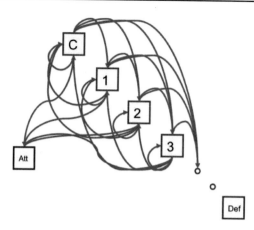

Figure 7.1. A visualization of the possible transitions between the various delinquency states. Only the transitions for the first few states are shown with the rest implied out through default.

Not all transitions are populated well enough to be modeled, even with the large dataset available. Table 7.1 shows the transition rates averaged across the full dataset. For this dataset, one forward transition and all backward transitions were modeled for each state. So the transitions from 2 to 3 months delinquent, 2 to 2, 2 to 1, 2 to Default, and 2 to Attrite are modeled, but 2 to 4 and 2 to 5 are not.

Pr(i->j) %	Current	1m Delq	2m Delq	3m Delq	4m Delq	5m Delq	Default	Attrite
Current	97.38%	0.88%	0.01%	0.00%	0.00%	0.00%	0.00%	1.73%
1m Delq	36.97%	44.88%	16.67%	0.09%	0.02%	0.00%	0.01%	1.35%
2m Delq	12.57%	16.48%	34.31%	35.44%	0.20%	0.03%	0.02%	0.90%
3m Delq	7.08%	3.64%	8.01%	20.45%	59.53%	0.21%	0.08%	0.83%
4m Delq	7.13%	1.14%	1.38%	3.49%	15.32%	69.88%	0.28%	0.80%
5m Delq	6.71%	0.78%	0.51%	0.78%	2.35%	12.46%	74.26%	0.77%

Table 7.1. Average transition probabilities between all possible states over the full dataset.

The transitions with enough data are modeled via logistic regression as monthly probabilities dependent upon macroeconomic factors, loan level factors, and transformations of the age of the loan, namely age, age^2, $\log(age)$, $\log^2(age)$. When the model for a transition is created, if some factors have insignificant coefficients, the least significant is removed and the estimation is repeated until all factors are significant. A binned factor is considered significant so long as it has one significant bin, because the zero level for the bins, and thus the reference point for the p-value estimation, is arbitrary.

Note that multinomial logistic regression is a preferable approach to estimating a set of logistic regression models for the transitions from a given state to all other possible states. However, multinomial logistic regression required so much memory (estimating many transitions simultaneously) that the dataset had to be reduced to the point where some of the transitions became unstable for modeling. The above approach is therefore a compromise for available resources.

The complete transition modeling approach used here is possible because of the large dataset, but also results in a large number of parameters. Practitioners often simplify the process by making assumptions about relationships between the transitions. As seen in Figure 7.2, the transitions do show a pattern, but not that of a simple distribution. For the current study, no further simplifications were explored, but the structure seen would justify such efforts.

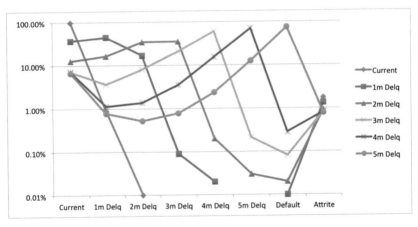

Figure 7.2. A graph of the transitions in Table 7.1 from each active state to all possible future states. The lines are the active states and the points are transitions to future states.

Figure 7.2 graphs the transition probabilities. Each line in the graph is a starting state, showing the transition probabilities to all other states. These lines represent highly non-normal, asymmetric distributions. The transformation from one distribution to the next can be visualized, but is not as easily captured mathematically. For balance dynamics, the scheduled payment according to the amortization schedule, Equation 1.5, is used as a baseline, and then a surplus payment rate is estimated collectively for all accounts.

$$\text{Oustanding Balance}(t) = \text{Outstanding Balance}(t-1) - \\ \text{Scheduled Principal Payment}(t) - \text{Surplus Principal Payment}(t) \quad (7.1)$$

The surplus principal payment is obtained by modeling

$$\text{Surplus Payment Rate}(t) = \frac{\text{Surplus Principal Payment}(t)}{\text{Scheduled Principal Payment}(t)} \quad (7.2)$$

The surplus payment rate is modeled the same as the delinquency state transitions, but with the assumption of a lognormal distribution.

7.1 Model Coefficients

To simplify the model estimation, the roll rate model macroeconomic factors were included without further optimizing the transformations. Forward transitions closely approximate roll rates, so this is a reasonable assumption. A further assumption was made that backward transitions would have the opposite macroeconomic sensitivity as the forward transitions, but possibly with different sensitivities.

One key point of discussion in state transition models is whether to forecast the input behavioral variables. For example, in a credit card model, utilization and payment rates change with time, and so one could ask if those factors should also be predicted as inputs to the model. For the state transition created here for mortgage, the only predictive factors were delinquency (by design) and origination factors. Although number of delinquencies in the last 6 months (for example) was tested, it was not found to be predictive. Therefore, we avoid the question about whether to forecast the input factors, because all selected factors are static with time.

Tables 7.2 – 7.4 show which factors were included in which models, marked with an "X". Some patterns are immediately clear. Age is the age of the account (not the person). This includes Age, Age^2, $ln(Age)$, and $ln(Age)^2$. These Age factors approximate a lifecycle function for each transition, and are found to be broadly useful. Property Type is always useful. # of Borrowers, LTV (Loan-to-Value Ratio), and Origination Balance are useful in most cases. Purpose is unused for subprime, but generally useful for prime and superprime. For subprime, DTI (Debt-to-Income Ratio) is useful only in a specific set of transformations—predicting the probability of transitioning one month forward in delinquency. For prime and superprime, DTI is more generally useful. For subprime and prime, Occupancy was only useful to predict that the account would transition to one month greater delinquency. Original Interest Rate was only predictive in superprime modeling.

Transition	Age	Property Type	# of Borrowers	Pur-pose	LTV	DTI	Orig Bal	Occu-pancy	Orig IR
0 to 0	X	X	X		X		X		
0 to 1	X	X	X		X	X	X	X	
0 to Attr	X	X	X		X		X		
1 to 0	X	X	X		X		X		
1 to 1	X	X	X		X		X		
1 to 2	X	X	X		X	X	X	X	
1 to Attr	X	X	X		X		X		
2 to 0	X	X			X		X		
2 to 1	X	X	X		X		X		
2 to 2	X	X	X				X		
2 to 3	X	X	X		X	X	X		X
2 to Attr	X	X			X		X		
3 to 0	X	X	X		X		X		
3 to 1	X	X			X		X		
3 to 2	X	X	X		X		X		
3 to 3	X	X	X		X		X		
3 to 4	X	X	X		X		X	X	
3 to 5	X	X			X				
4 to 0	X	X	X		X		X		
4 to 1		X			X		X		
4 to 2		X					X		
4 to 3	X	X	X		X		X		
4 to 4	X	X	X				X		
4 to 5	X	X	X		X		X	X	
4 to Attr	X	X			X				
5 to 0		X			X		X		
5 to 1		X	X		X				
5 to 2	X	X							
5 to 3	X	X			X		X		
5 to 4	X	X							
5 to 5	X	X			X		X		
5 to Def	X	X	X		X		X	X	
5 to Attr		X			X				

Table 7.2. The Xs show which input factors were used to model each transition rate for the subprime segment.

State	Age	Property Type	# of Borrowers	Pur-pose	LTV	DTI	Orig Bal	Occu-pancy	Orig IR
0 to 0	X	X	X	X	X	X	X		
0 to 1	X	X	X	X	X	X	X	X	
0 to Attr	X	X	X	X	X	X	X		
1 to 0	X	X	X	X	X	X	X		
1 to 1	X	X		X	X	X	X		
1 to 2	X	X	X	X	X	X	X	X	
1 to Attr	X	X	X	X	X	X	X		
2 to 0	X	X	X	X	X	X	X		
2 to 1	X	X	X	X	X		X		
2 to 2	X	X	X	X	X	X	X		
2 to 3	X	X	X		X	X	X	X	
2 to Attr	X	X			X	X	X		
3 to 0		X					X		
3 to 1		X			X	X	X		
3 to 2	X	X			X	X	X		
3 to 3	X	X	X		X	X	X		
3 to 4	X	X	X		X			X	
3 to 5	X	X			X	X	X		
4 to 0		X		X					
4 to 1	X	X		X	X				
4 to 2	X	X							
4 to 3	X	X							
4 to 4	X	X	X	X		X	X		
4 to 5	X	X	X	X	X	X	X	X	
4 to Attr		X				X	X		
5 to 0		X		X			X		
5 to 1		X		X					
5 to 2		X							
5 to 3		X							
5 to 4	X	X			X		X		
5 to 5	X	X		X		X	X		
5 to Def	X	X	X	X	X	X	X	X	
5 to Attr		X		X	X		X		

Table 7.3. The Xs show which input factors were used to model each transition rate for the prime segment.

Tables 7.5 & 7.6 show coefficients for specific variables as used in the transition models for the subprime segment. In each case, the coefficients are reversed when predicting backward transitions as compared to forward transitions, as would be expected. While creating the models, filters were used to exclude factors that had the inconsistent signs

State	Age	Property Type	# of Borrowers	Purpose	LTV	DTI	Orig Bal	Occupancy	Orig IR
0 to 0	X	X	X	X	X	X	X	X	X
0 to 1	X	X	X		X	X	X		
0 to Attr	X	X	X	X	X	X	X	X	X
1 to 0	X	X	X	X	X	X		X	X
1 to 1	X	X	X	X	X	X	X	X	
1 to 2	X	X	X		X	X	X		
1 to Attr	X	X	X	X	X		X	X	
2 to 0	X	X			X	X	X		
2 to 1	X	X					X		X
2 to 2	X	X		X	X	X	X	X	
2 to 3	X	X			X		X		
2 to Attr	X	X		X	X				
3 to 0	X	X		X	X		X		
3 to 1	X	X					X		
3 to 2	X	X		X			X		
3 to 3		X		X			X	X	
3 to 4	X	X				X			
3 to 5	X	X				X			
4 to 0	X	X				X			
4 to 1		X							
4 to 2	X	X							
4 to 3		X							
4 to 4		X	X				X	X	X
4 to 5		X	X				X		
4 to Attr		X				X			
5 to 0		X					X	X	
5 to 1		X			X			X	
5 to 2		X							
5 to 3		X							
5 to 4	X	X					X		
5 to 5	X	X	X	X			X	X	
5 to Def	X	X				X	X		
5 to Attr	X	X				X			

Table 7.4. The Xs show which input factors were used to model each transition rate for the superprime segment.

for any of the levels. For example, if Property Type = Manufactured Housing was a positive risk indicator for one forward transition but a negative sign for another forward transition, then Property Type would be excluded as an unstable or inconsistent indicator.

From \To	1	2	3	4	5	6	Att	Def
0	−0.194	0.294						
1	−0.428		0.382				−0.427	
2	−0.340	−0.141	−0.069	0.397			−0.879	
3	−0.349	−0.296	−0.247	−0.097	0.347		−1.083	
4	−0.325	−0.466	−0.312	−0.157	−0.097	0.310	−1.255	
5	−0.190	−0.479	−0.505	−0.462	−0.135	−0.146	−1.390	0.311

Table 7.5. Coefficients for LTV in the transition models for the subprime segment.

Confidence intervals are not shown because of space limitations, but all of the coefficients shown were already required to pass a 95% confidence level. Of course, a formal model submission to examiners could have dozens of pages of coefficients and confidence intervals for a detailed review.

From \To	1	2	3	4	5	6	Att	Def
0	0.121	−0.218					0.167	
1	0.050	0.067	−0.204				0.197	
2	0.008	0.071	0.115	−0.137			0.112	
3	0.091	0.058	0.099	0.164	−0.160		0.085	
4	0.088	0.080	0.130	0.171	0.195	−0.179	0.093	
5	0.041	0.063	0.135	0.134	0.193	0.158	0.058	-0.134

Table 7.6. Coefficients for number of borrowers in the transition models for the subprime segment. One borrower has a zero coefficient. Two or more borrowers have the coefficients shown.

Higher origination LTV causes higher risk of forward transition. A nonlinear function of LTV was estimated, because the relationship between transition probability and LTV is not linear in LTV. Although not explored here, with sufficient data, one could consider having a different relationship between LTV and transition probability for forward and backward transitions, rather than simply inverting the relationship with a coefficient. Even with the amount of data available here, data gets thin quickly for the less common transitions.

Refreshed LTV was not available in the dataset. Analysts will sometimes try to create an approximate refreshed LTV using state or MSA-level house price index (HPI). That is not done here, because such estimates just create a parallel shift for all properties in the same region. The same information is captured simply by putting change in HPI in the model, which was offered as a candidate variable to all the models in the study.

For number of borrowers, more borrowers reduces the likelihood of forward transitions and increases backward transitions. This appears be the effect of borrowing jointly with a spouse or parent.

Table 7.7 shows the coefficients for use of Debt-to-income ratio (DTI) for the prime segment. As with the two previous tables, each coefficient was estimated independently in a completely separate regression model. Only statistically significant coefficients were retained in the models, but where retained they show a remarkable consistency.

From \To	1	2	3	4	5	6	Att	Def
0	−0.413	1.556						
1	−0.676		0.277				−0.037	
2	−0.526	−0.204		0.065				
3	−0.285	−0.381	−0.143				−0.226	
4	−0.072	−0.315	−0.144				−0.181	
5							−0.213	

Table 7.7. Coefficients for Debt to Income ratio (DTI) in the transition models for the prime segment.

7.1.1 Models by US state

The same state transition modeling approach was employed independently in each of the 52 states and territories, creating 52 states and territories ×3 risk segments ×33 transitions = 5,148 independent logistic regression models. Obviously, fully automated procedures were used to generate the models. As before, variable selection was rerun separately for each state with factors excluded based upon insignificance or inconsistency.

Tables 7.8 – 7.10 show the frequency of factor selection for the three separate risk grades across the 52 state models. As can be seen in the tables, LTV, Number of Borrowers (1 or 2+), and Original Balance are the three most frequently significant factors. DTI, Loan Purpose, Occupancy, and Property Type appear in some models. This gives an idea of the relative importance of these factors to the forecast when considered across the 4,950 separate models.

From \To	LTV	# of Borrowers	Orig Balance	DTI	Loan Purpose	Occu-pancy	Property Type
0 to 0	43	51	45				
0 to 1	44	52	18	47		47	
0 to Attr	3	51	8				6
1 to 0	45	25	44				
1 to 1	4	48	3				1
1 to 2	28	51	37	38			
1 to Attr	22	38	28				1
2 to 0	42	3	48				
2 to 1	24	21	48				2
2 to 2	10	45					7
2 to 3	43	45	46	31			
2 to Attr	38	7	11				2
3 to 0	30	13	25				
3 to 1	28	4	31				
3 to 2	22	16	16				1
3 to 3	6	43	1				2
3 to 4	32	46	23	12		1	
3 to Attr	36	5	10				
4 to 0	30	10	11				1
4 to 1	16	1	10				
4 to 2	7	6	13				
4 to 3	9	16	4				
4 to 4	5	40	2				2
4 to 5	27	41	9	2			
4 to Attr	36	4	6				
5 to 0	25	9	9				
5 to 1	10		6				
5 to 2	6	1	3				
5 to 3	9	3	4				
5 to 4	6	8	3				1
5 to 5	8	28					3
5 to Attr	29	1	6				1
5 to Def	22	29	7	3			

Table 7.8. The numbers indicate how many of the 52 US state models used a given input factor for the subprime segment.

7.2 Forecasting

Under the Markov criteria, if the forecast requires no information about the history of the transitions, then a simple matrix multiply may

From \To	LTV	Num Borrowers	Orig Balance	DTI	Loan Purpose	Occupancy	Property Type
0 to 0	51	31	42	52	40		
0 to 1	52	52	9	52		28	
0 to Attr	14	52	3	12			5
1 to 0	52	46	26	52			
1 to 1		20	5		32		3
1 to 2	48	51	35	49	2	1	
1 to Attr	30	47	25	19			
2 to 0	46	5	47	45			
2 to 1	15	12	39	10	1		2
2 to 2	3	38	1		25		5
2 to 3	32	42	35	6	4		
2 to Attr	40	11	16	2			
3 to 0	27	6	24	4	1		
3 to 1	13	4	27	10	1		
3 to 2	12	7	12	3	1		
3 to 3	4	35	1		19		5
3 to 4	29	40	11	1	7		
3 to Attr	35	2	12	4	1		
4 to 0	14	6	8	2	3		1
4 to 1	6	4	8	4			1
4 to 2	3	1	5	3	1		
4 to 3	7	12	2	1	4		
4 to 4	6	26	1		21		2
4 to 5	21	31	2	1	10		
4 to Attr	34	4	8	4			1
5 to 0	8	3	3	2			
5 to 1	11	1	6	2	2		
5 to 2	8	2	5	1	4		1
5 to 3	5	2	3	1	4		
5 to 4	1	11			5		1
5 to 5	5	23		1	13		5
5 to Attr	37	3	9	4			
5 to Def	16	23	2	1	5		

Table 7.9. The numbers indicate how many of the 52 US state models used a given input factor for the prime segment.

be used for forecasting. In the current context where the states are delin-quency buckets, if the previous delinquency history is predictive, then a very computationally intensive Monte Carlo simulation approach must be used. A common example of an input factor that violates the Markov

From \To	LTV	Num Borrowers	Orig Balance	DTI	Loan Purpose	Occu-pancy	Property Type
0 to 0			51	47	46	6	
0 to 1	50	52	6	52			
0 to Attr	16	52					11
1 to 0	49	45	13	52		5	
1 to 1	1	4	13		5	7	1
1 to 2	47	50	16	37			
1 to Attr	25	21	12	9	2		
2 to 0	36	3	11	19	1	3	1
2 to 1	6	3	22	2	1	5	3
2 to 2	2	17		1	5	8	2
2 to 3	26	13	22	2			
2 to Attr	25	7	8	9	3	1	
3 to 0	15	2	5				
3 to 1	2	2	8	1			
3 to 2	5	3	3	2	3	5	
3 to 3	2	17	1	2	5	1	1
3 to 4	24	14	6	3			
3 to Attr	15	1	3	3	4	1	
4 to 0	11	4	3	2			
4 to 1	5	1					
4 to 2		3					
4 to 3	5	2	1				1
4 to 4	3	12		2	10		2
4 to 5	19	13	3	3			
4 to Attr	21	2	5	1	1	1	
5 to 0	12	2	2	3			
5 to 1	3	1		1			1
5 to 2	1	1	1	1			1
5 to 3	5	3	1	1	1	1	
5 to 4	1	1	1		2	1	
5 to 5	2	5	1	2	3		2
5 to Attr	17	3	3	1			
5 to Def	10	8	1	3			

Table 7.10. The numbers indicate how many of the 52 US state and territory models used a given input factor for the superprime segment.

criterion would be the number of times delinquent in the previous six months. Although sensible as a predictive factor, that proved to be re-dundant with other factors that satisfy the Markov criterion. Therefore, simple matrix multiplies were used for the forecasting. The final forecast was a set of expectation values for the number of accounts in each state rather than a discrete number of accounts arising from Monte Carlo simulation.

Figure 7.3 shows how the population density with state evolves versus forecast horizon when the economic factors were held flat and the seasonality is set to zero. Since no new loan originations are being considered, the fraction that is Current (0 months delinquent) drains slowly into the delinquency buckets or prepayment. As a percentage of total active accounts, the delinquency buckets rise. The later buckets and default reach saturation levels.

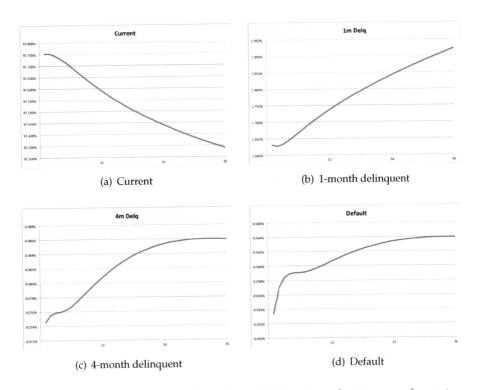

(a) Current

(b) 1-month delinquent

(c) 4-month delinquent

(d) Default

Figure 7.3. Graphs showing the portion of the loans in each state versus forecast horizon.

The loan-level state transition dynamics cause the interesting behavior in the first few months of Figure 7.3. Thereafter, the evolution is driven by the gradual pay-off and default of the loans.

Figure 7.4 shows that macroeconomic drivers create all of the long-term dynamics in the population. When real economic conditions for the recession and recovery are used, the dynamics for the flat economic conditions are minimal in comparison. This simply shows that the portfolio totals reflect the mean of the distribution of account probabilities. The

Figure 7.4. Graphs showing the portion of the loans in each state versus forecast horizon under three scenarios.

mean is driven by economics and lifecycle (in the vintage model) and variations in underwriting, but behavioral information does not much affect the mean beyond the first few months.

The primary reason that the state transition models did not perform well over long horizons is that the coefficients are mostly capturing short-term dynamics. The long-term extrapolation behavior is not well defined in the estimation process. That would require making the coefficients functions of forecast horizon, which the author has not seen done in such models, although it certainly could be.

7.3 Possible Enhancements

State transition models probably have the greatest number of possible variations of any in this study. The challenge is how to make tradeoffs between the amount of data and the number of coefficients. Perhaps the most common is to model the probability of moving one up or one down the delinquency chain.

Each transition is really just another rate to be modeled, so any of the techniques described here to be used. For example, a vintage model or a discrete time survival model could be used to model each of the transitions, or at least the most important ones. Because of all the hybridization, modeling techniques can start to blur together. Boundaries and definitions can be difficult.

8

Discrete Time Survival Models

Survival models (Cox and Oakes 1984) are related to vintage models, but usually with the implication of creating loan-level models with scoring attributes. Cox proportional hazards models (Cox 1972) are the original and classic approach to creating such models, but they were developed with continuous time in mind. For monthly sampled data such as is available here and in lending in general, discrete time survival models are employed.

Once the change to discrete time is made, the result is just a logistic regression panel model of probability of default (PD) or probability of attrition (PA). Practitioners commonly include age as a factor in the regression, either nonparametrically or as a set of transformations as shown in the state transition model. Transformations of macroeconomic factors and scoring factors are included as well. Then a regression solve is performed.

Because of problems with multicolinearity between age of the account, macroeconomic factors, and behavioral scoring factors (Breeden and Thomas 2016), this study follows a modified approach developed by Breeden (Breeden 2016) which takes the lifecycle and environment functions from the vintage model as fixed inputs.

This approach reduces the colinearity problem by using the known dynamics for lifecycle and environment. Behavioral factors like delinquency, utilization, etc. naturally exhibit colinearity to age of the loan and macroeconomic factors, because such behavioral factors are themselves dependent upon loan age and macroeconomic factors. By pre-estimating the macroeconomic and lifecycle sensitivities with the vintage model and including them in the model with fixed coefficients, the behavioral factors essentially model the residuals. This concentrates the population dynamics into the lifecycle and environment functions and leaves the scoring factors as loan-level idiosyncratic effects, thereby creating a solution to the multicolinearity problem and eliminating any need to forecast the behavioral factors.

Separate origination and behavioral models are built, the former using only factors available at origination and the latter using both origination factors and behavioral factors such as recent delinquency.

$$\log\left(\frac{p_i(a,v,t,h)}{1-p_i(a,v,t,h)}\right) = F(a) + H(t) + c_{0,h} + \sum_{j=1}^{n_s} c_{j,h}s_{ij} + \sum_{v=1}^{n_v} g_v \qquad (8.1)$$

For the behavioral models, the approach shown here, Equation 8.1 estimates coefficients, $c_{j,h}$, as a function of forecast horizon, h, because the information value decays at different rates for different behavioral factors, s_{ij}. The coefficients at each forecast horizon are estimated via a separate regression. This is not the standard discrete time survival model, but really a multi-horizon discrete time survival model. Without the multi-horizon aspect, many practitioners would lag the delinquency factors by six months or so, in order to have better long-term robustness, but at the price of near-term accuracy. The multi-horizon enhancement seeks to obtain both near-term and long-term accuracy.

The dummy variables g_v quantify any residual, vintage-specific credit risk not captured in the scoring factors.

Loan-level estimates of PD and PA were created by the process above. EAD followed the same process, but with a lognormal distribution.

8.1 Model Coefficients

The plots and tables in this section provide an overview of the factors included in the discrete time survival model. This model is a single-step-to-PD approach, rather than the bucket-by-bucket approach of the state transition model. However, the factors that are predictive for forward transitions in the state transition model are also predictive in the PD model.

The lifecycle function and macroeconomic factors (environment function) are the same here as for the vintage model, so those components can be seen in the vintage model discussion. The only addition to the model is in coefficients for the behavioral factors.

8.1.1 Probability of default

The coefficients are functions of forecast horizon, meaning that the importance to the forecast depends upon how far into the future one is trying predict. Figure 8.1 is the best example of this. When trying to predict one month forward, severe delinquency is the strongest predictor of default. An account that is 2 months delinquent at the start of the forecast has the greatest risk of default at horizon 4. For all delinquencies states, the predictive value declines dramatically beyond 6 months into the future, because delinquent accounts will most likely have either cured or defaulted by then. In fact, the most severely delinquent accounts (5 months delinquent in this analysis) are less likely to default at horizon 6 than a less delinquent account. This is because any 5-month delinquent accounts that are still active by 6 months into the future must have cured and therefore are not such a severed default risk.

All of the delinquency coefficients are measured relative to nondelinquent accounts, which are thus assigned a coefficient of 0. This means that any delinquent account is more risky than a non-delinquent account, but the relationship for delinquent accounts is highly nonlinear.

Figure 8.2 shows the coefficients for some of the other variables in the scores. Note that in the first few months of the forecast, the other candidate variables make almost no contribution to the forecast—delinquency is everything. As the predictive value of delinquency diminishes around horizon 6, the other factors take over. By horizon 12, the coefficients have almost converged to the values that appear in the origination score, meaning that for long-range forecasting, origination information still dominates behavioral information. This is probably not true for credit cards, where the transactor / revolver distinction is critical for the entire forecast.

The model is already segmented by FICO, so it does not appear directly in the model. We tested it, but it was no longer significant beyond the initial segmentation.

Figure 8.3 shows the coefficients for annual vintage dummy variables. Note that the Superprime line is the most volatile, because the fewest number of defaults were available for the modeling.

Compare these to Figure 6.2, which is the full vintage credit risk in the vintage model without adjustment for known factors like LTV, DTI, or delinquency. The vintage residuals show that much of the vintage structure persists. This suggests that the credit cycle is more than just lenders changing their origination criteria. Previous research by (Breeden and Canals-Cerdá 2016) found the same result on a broader

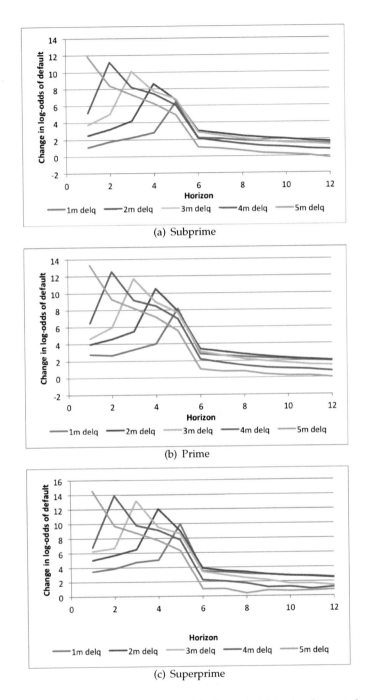

Figure 8.1. Coefficients predicting default probability by forecast horizon (months) for each delinquency state.

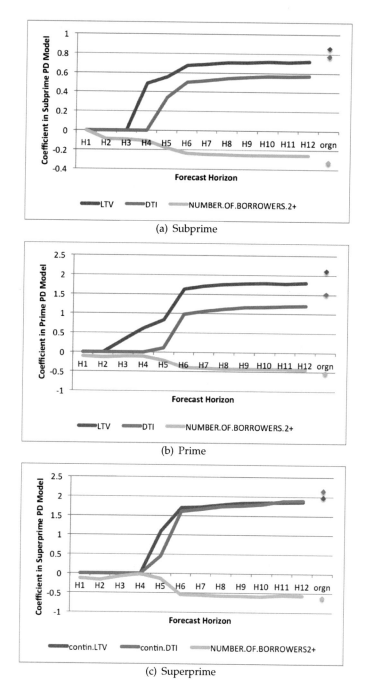

Figure 8.2. Coefficients predicting default probability by forecast horizon (months) or origination score for some key predictive factors.

dataset including securitized pool performance. That study concluded that the residual structure was likely due to consumer risk appetite correlated to the economic cycle, also referred to as macroeconomic adverse selection. Consumer loan demand in the Senior Loan Officer Opinion Survey (SLOOS) correlated well in that study, and would also correlate well to the vintage residuals here.

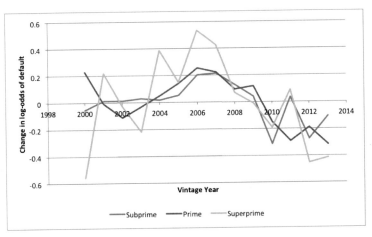

Figure 8.3. Vintage residuals in the PD behavior scores.

In addition to the factors shown here, the PD models for subprime and superprime also included origination balance. The model for prime included origination balance, loan purpose, and occupancy status.

8.1.2 Probability of attrition

Probability of attrition was modeled using the same process as probability of default. Unlike with PD, PA did not find significant value in delinquency except for subprime. Also, delinquency's impact was much more steady and long-lasting, Figure 8.4. The higher the delinquency at the start of the forecast, the lower the attrition probability. The effect is probably that it reduces the opportunity to refinance. Delinquency did not appear at all in the prime or superprime models.

Most attrition is assumed to be driven by changes in interest rates. Part of that is already captured by the environment function, which correlates to changes in interest rates. However, interest rates were also tested in a different way as an explanatory factor in the PA behavior score. The most interesting measure would be to compare the origination interest rate for the loan to what that borrower could obtain in a refinancing. However, we do not know what interest rate they would

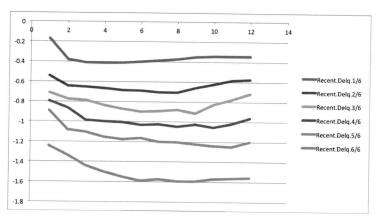

Figure 8.4. Coefficients by delinquency for subprime for predicting probability of attrition.

obtain. In previous work, we have built a model to predict what the refinance interest rate would be and compare that to the origination interest rate as a scoring factor. Although it sounds good, in practice it was not measurably better than comparing the average origination interest rate for the vintage of this loan to the average origination interest rate for a new vintage at the later date to be tested.

Figure 8.5 shows the coefficients for the change in new loan interest rates between a given loan's origination date and the forecast start date. Coefficients are not shown for prime, because they were not significant for that segment, presumably because of redundancy with other information in the model. The graphs show that as the delta between origination and current interest rates increases, the likelihood of attrition increases—up to a point. For subprime loans, this peaks and starts to decline, suggesting loans that received higher rates because they were higher risk and cannot refinance at lower rates.

Without the strong delinquency dynamic, the other coefficients were more stable with forecast horizon. Figure 8.6 shows some of these coefficients for subprime, prime, and superprime. As observed for PD, the coefficients for long horizons generally converge to the values used in the origination score that had no behavioral information.

8.1.3 Models by US state

The above process was applied independently to 50 US states, Puerto Rico and Guam. The lifecycle and environment functions from the state-level vintage models were taken as inputs. Then the behavior scores

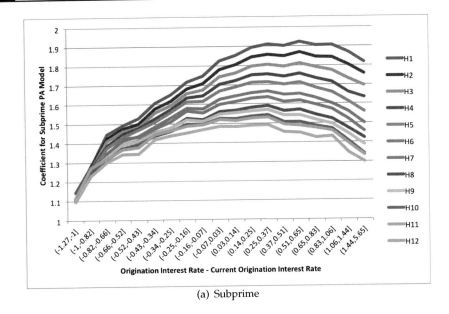

(a) Subprime

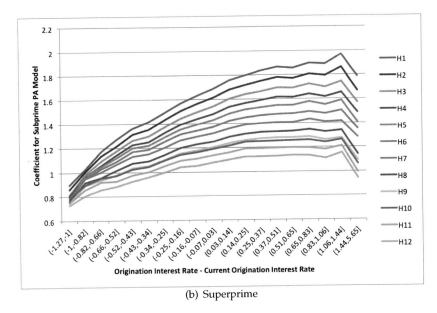

(b) Superprime

Figure 8.5. Coefficients for change in interest rates for probability of attrition.

were estimated. Tables 8.1 – 8.3 show the usage frequency by state, which largely mirrors the usage in the national models.

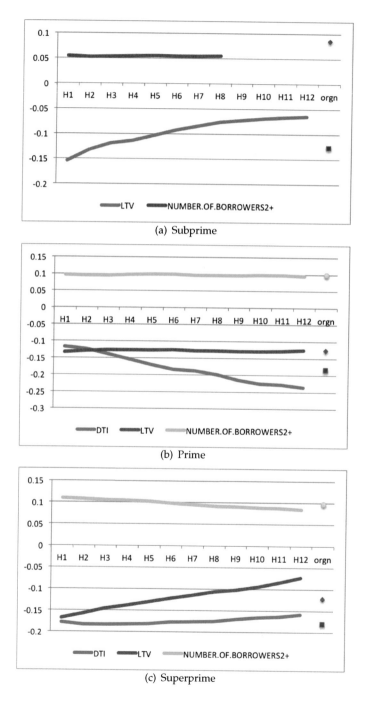

(a) Subprime

(b) Prime

(c) Superprime

Figure 8.6. Coefficients for predictive factors for probability of attrition.

Variable	H1	H2	H3	H4	H5	H6	H7	H8	H9	H10	H11	H12	Orig
DTI	46	46	46	46	46	46	46	46	46	46	46	46	46
LTV	52	52	52	52	52	52	52	52	52	52	52	52	52
Origination.Balance	39	39	39	39	39	39	39	39	39	39	39	39	39
Delinquency	52	52	52	52	52	52	52	52	52	52	52	52	52
Number of Borrowers	52	52	52	52	52	52	52	52	52	52	52	52	52
Occupancy Status	15	15	15	15	15	15	15	15	15	15	15	15	15
Annual Vintage	52	52	52	52	52	52	52	52	52	52	52	52	52

Table 8.1. The numbers indicate how many of the 52 US state and territorial models used a given input factor for the subprime segment.

Variable	H1	H2	H3	H4	H5	H6	H7	H8	H9	H10	H11	H12	Orig
DTI	52	52	52	52	52	52	52	52	52	52	52	52	52
LTV	52	52	52	52	52	52	52	52	52	52	52	52	52
Origination.Balance	34	34	34	34	34	34	34	34	34	34	34	34	34
Delinquency	52	52	52	52	52	52	52	52	52	52	52	52	52
Number of Borrowers	52	52	52	52	52	52	52	52	52	52	52	52	52
Occupancy Status	18	18	18	18	18	18	18	18	18	18	18	18	18
Annual Vintage	52	52	52	52	52	52	52	52	52	52	52	52	52

Table 8.2. The numbers indicate how many of the 52 US state and territorial models used a given input factor for the prime segment.

Variable	H1	H2	H3	H4	H5	H6	H7	H8	H9	H10	H11	H12	Orig
DTI	50	50	50	50	50	50	50	50	50	50	50	50	50
LTV	52	52	52	52	52	52	52	52	52	52	52	52	52
Origination.Balance	9	9	9	9	9	9	9	9	9	9	9	9	9
Delinquency	52	52	52	52	52	52	52	52	52	52	52	52	52
Number of Borrowers	51	51	51	51	51	51	51	51	51	51	51	51	51
Annual Vintage	52	52	52	52	52	52	52	52	52	52	52	52	52

Table 8.3. The numbers indicate how many of the 52 US state and territorial models used a given input factor for the superprime segment.

State-level probability of attrition models were also created, again with results similar to the national models.

8.2 Forecasting

The forecasting operates at the loan level to predict the expectation values of default and attrition according to Equation 8.1. The PD and PA models predict the conditional probabilities, so the monthly unconditional expectations are obtained as

$$PD_{unconditional} = PD_{conditional} \prod_{i=1}^{h-1} \left(1 - PD_{conditional}(i) - PA_{conditional}(i)\right) \qquad (8.2)$$

Unconditional PA is computed similarly to Equation 8.2.

The default balances are computed the same as for the state transition model in Equations 7.1 & 7.2. That involves reducing the balance each month by the scheduled principal payment and then adding a surplus payment amount according to the model of surplus payment rate. The final lifetime loss forecasts are created by aggregating the loan-level monthly loss estimates of expected default balances.

Although model results are shown for origination scores, new originations are not considered under CECL. The origination model details are shown only for comparison purposes and are not part of the forecasts created here.

8.2.1 Validation results

For model validation in addition to the cross-model comparisons in Chapter 2, the following statistics measure the account discrimination power and in-sample fit of the models.

Figures 8.7 & 8.8 show the KS and Gini coefficients for the models. The discrimination power of the origination and behavioral models over a 12-month forecast horizon. As expected, the behavior scores have more discrimination power, particularly where delinquency matters most.

Because different coefficients are estimated for each forecast horizon through the first 12 months, the discrimination power can be measured separately for each forecast month. Those results are shown in Figure 8.9. As expected, the discrimination power is greatest in the first five months of the forecast where delinquency is dominant. By the twelfth month, the discrimination power is converging to that of the origination score, the same way the coefficient estimates converge to the origination score coefficients.

Figures 8.10 & 8.11 show the discrimination power of the probability of attrition models. As expected, attrition is much more difficult to predict than default. Part of this comes from the relative unimportance of delinquency, but all factors are less predictive for attrition.

When looking by forecast horizon, Figure 8.12, the performance is quite stable with forecast horizon, again because of the limited role of delinquency in the forecasts. The primary forecasting factors for attrition have a slow decay rate for the information value.

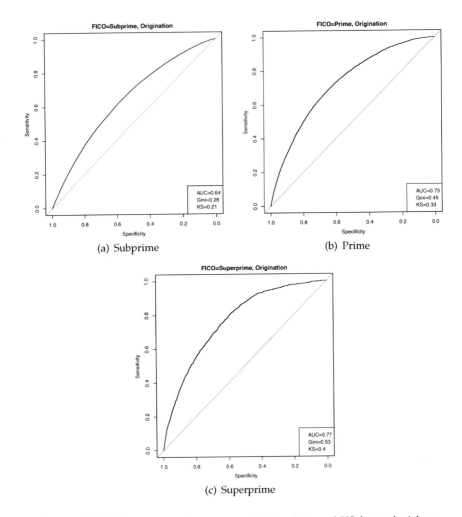

Figure 8.7. ROC graphs and measures of AUC, Gini, and KS for each risk segment for the PD origination score.

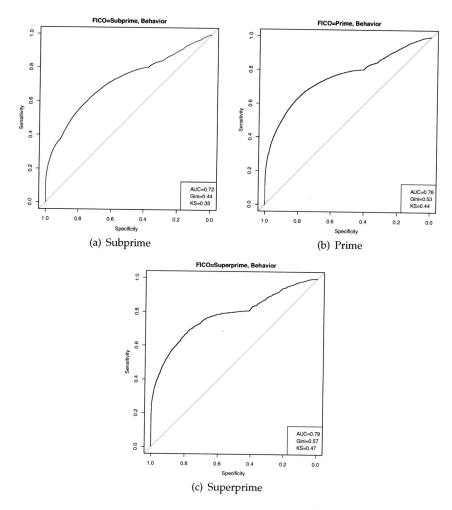

Figure 8.8. ROC graphs and measures of AUC, Gini, and KS for each risk segment for the PD behavior score.

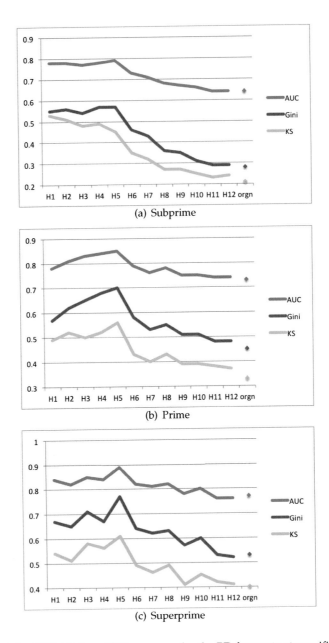

Figure 8.9. AUC, Gini, and KS measures for the PD forecasts at specific forecast horizons.

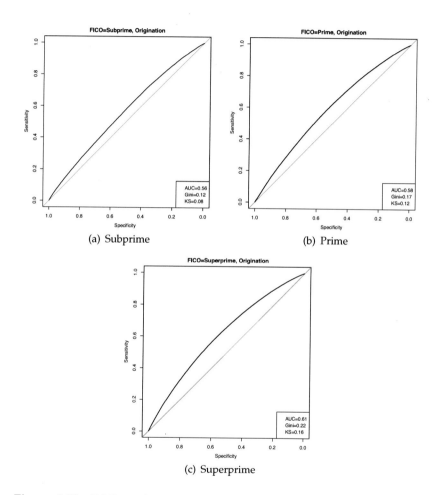

(a) Subprime

(b) Prime

(c) Superprime

Figure 8.10. ROC graphs and measures of AUC, Gini, and KS for each risk segment for the PA origination score.

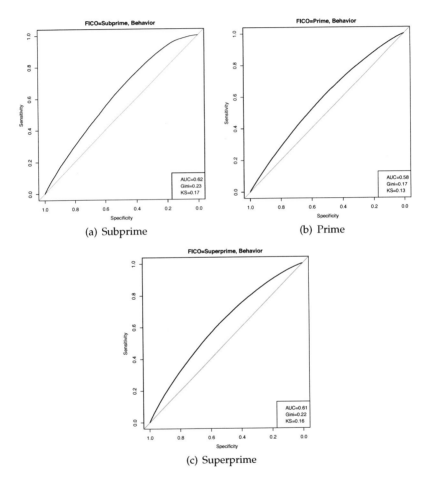

Figure 8.11. ROC graphs and measures of AUC, Gini, and KS for each risk segment for the PA behavior score.

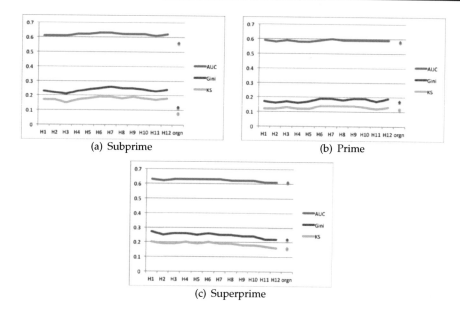

(a) Subprime

(b) Prime

(c) Superprime

Figure 8.12. AUC, Gini, and KS measures for the PA forecasts at specific forecast horizons.

All of these results confirm that the multi-horizon discrete time survival model performs well and is a powerful approach for lifetime loss estimates such as required for CECL.

8.3 Possible Enhancements

The use of separate coefficients by forecast horizon already represents a significant enhancement over the standard approach to discrete time survival models. However, additional enhancements are still possible. When modeling the probability of attrition, the available information about change in interest rates or change in property values between origination and the current point might argue for a modified structure. One could retain the lifecycle function that is an average through all economic conditions, but replace the environment and vintage functions simultaneously with these measures of change since origination. Then vintage and environment dummies or factors could still be included, but they might not have the same magnitude as they would have had in the current approach.

9

Models Not Considered

The models shown in this study to not encompass all possible model types for mortgage. Beyond the variations and hybrids possible for the methods list above, some approaches were either impossible or unreasonable.

9.1 Historic Precedent

The CECL rules seek to make the process simpler for smaller institutions. The first example provided in the guidelines describes how one might approximate lifetime losses for a 10-year fixed term loan. Their suggestion is to find a similar loan or segment in a previous time period for which the full lifetime loss is known, then make an adjustment for the current environment and apply the resulting loss rate to the current loans.

Although seemingly simple, the details can actually be challenging. Few portfolios would have the 10 years of history necessary for the look-up table approach described above. The same is true here. For 30-year fixed term mortgages in the Fannie Mae and Freddie Mac data, full lifetime losses are not present in the historic data. Of course, models are employed when data alone cannot provide an answer, but to see how simple we can make things, the historic precedent model described here uses as little modeling as possible.

The current dataset provides enough history to measure the loss experience for a 10-year span. Using this, the 10-year cumulative loss rate for loans originated in 2005 could be aggregated. This period covers the recession roughly equally, and thus might be considered a through-the-cycle average for an average risk vintage. However, to get to lifetime loss, a residual risk estimate is required. For that, the performance for the loans between 109 and 120 months-on-book could be aggregated to create a conditional balance default rate, $DR_{\text{last year}}$.

$$\text{Cumulative } DR_{10 \text{ year}} = \frac{\sum_{a=0}^{119} \text{Default Balance}(a)}{\text{Booked Volume}} \tag{9.1}$$

$$\text{Cumulative } DR_{\text{last year}} = \frac{\sum_{a=108}^{119} \text{Default Balance}(a)}{\text{Outstanding Balance}(a = 107)} \tag{9.2}$$

Unlike all of the models in the study, this approach does not explicitly consider the competing risks of prepayment and default. Instead, they are combined by looking simply at the lifetime loss rates as a percentage of all originated loans. Prepayment is implied in the loss rate.

Combining the measured balance default rate from the first 10 years and the approximate losses for the subsequent years yields

$$DR_{\text{lifetime}} = DR_{10 \text{ year}} + \sum_{i=10}^{29} \frac{B_i}{B_0} PD_{\text{last year}} \tag{9.3}$$

$$\frac{B_i}{B_0} = \frac{(1+r)^N - (1+r)^i}{(1+r)^N - 1} \tag{9.4}$$

where B_0 is the initial loan amount, r is the monthly interest rate, and N is the term of the loan in months. For $N = 360$, this simplifies to the following.

$$\sum_{y=10}^{29} \frac{B_i}{B_0} = 55.8r + 7.1 \tag{9.5}$$

and therefore

$$PD_{\text{lifetime}} = PD_{10 \text{ year}} + (55.8r + 7.1)PD_{\text{last year}} \tag{9.6}$$

Basically, the estimate for the out-years just applies the last year default rate to the amortization schedule, thus assuming no prepayment in those years. This formula contains many approximations, but is simple to implement. Obviously, the statement about no prepayment means that it should significantly over-estimate the loss rate in those years.

The final adjustment is for the foreseeable economic future from a specific starting point. Because of the data range chosen above, Equation 9.6 is roughly a through-the-cycle (TTC) average for 30-year mortgage performance. If the economic adjustment is to be done without modeling, it requires an assessment by management to determine whether near-future economic conditions will raise or lower the default rate during that period relative to the TTC average. Most likely this would be done by comparing the conditions of an economic scenario to a similar period in the last economic cycle and computing an appropriate increment.

For the current study, this was all too approximate to be considered a model. Clearly, the idea of using previous lifetime loss experiences will work best for shorter term loans. For loans and portfolios where the full term experience is not present in the historical data, a better quality model is advised.

9.2 Grade Migration

Probably the most popular approach not included in this study is Grade Migration. Of course, roll rates and state transition models are forms of grade migration, but the term usually carries a different connotation. For commercial loans, grades are usually risk grades provided by the rating agencies or an equivalent in-house model used to assess the financial health of the borrower. Migration would mean downgrades leading to loan default.

In the context of mortgages or consumer loans generally, "grade" usually refers to FICO scores or an equivalent in-house score. However, unlike the grades from rating agencies, FICO scores do not carry an implied default probability. Instead, one must create an estimate of probability of default given a FICO score, an economic scenario, and a specific loan type. Therefore, a grade migration model for retail loan loans means creating two models: one model predicts the changes in FICO scores over time with changes in economic conditions and the other model predicts the probability of default from any given score, also given economic conditions.

Although FICO score is used in all of the models in the study, either for risk segmentation or for loan-level modeling, it is always the FICO score at origination. In this dataset, no refreshed FICO scores were available, so grade migration could not be tested.

PART III

Background

10

Mean-Reverting Scenarios

Generating mean-reverting scenarios is important to implementing all of the models in the study. This proved to be surprisingly difficult, not in generating the scenarios, but in doing so in a way that would create comparable scenarios for any of the models regardless of how the macroeconomic data was used. After much experimentation, the fairest approach was found to be to collect the macroeconomic factors of a given rate being modeled, after transformation and coefficient estimation, into a single index. This index would represent the full economic sensitivity of that rate, essentially the same as the environment function n the vintage model. A mean reverting scenario was applied to that index returning it to a through-the-cycle average. The relaxation rate was determined from the history and set the same for all models.

10.1 Ornstein-Uhlenbeck Process

The creation of mean-reverting scenarios for credit risk modeling has been described previously by Breeden and Liang (Breeden and Liang 2015). The following summarizes how mean-reverting models could be created using an Ornstein-Uhlenbeck process (Uhlenbeck and Ornstein 1930).

The Ornstein-Uhlenbeck process is a continuous-time stochastic process often described in the context of Brownian motion.

$$dx_t = \theta(\mu - x_t)dt + \sigma dW_t \tag{10.1}$$

For a studied property x_t, μ is the long-run mean of the process, θ is related to the relaxation time, and σ is related to the variance.

In discrete time, the O-U process simplifies to a structured AR(1) process.

$$\Delta x(t) = \theta(\mu - x(t))\Delta t + \epsilon_t \tag{10.2}$$

where

$$\mu = d - \frac{\sigma^2}{2\theta}, \quad \epsilon_t \approx N(0,\sigma). \tag{10.3}$$

Given this process, the expected mean and variance are

$$E(x(t)) = \left(1 - e^{-\theta(t-t_0)}\right)\mu + e^{-\theta(t-t_0)}x(t_0) \tag{10.4}$$

$$\text{Var}(x(t)) = \frac{\sigma^2}{2\theta}\left(1 - e^{-2\theta(t-t_0)}\right) \tag{10.5}$$

In the limit as $t \to \infty$, this becomes

$$\lim_{t \to \infty} E(x(t)) = \mu \tag{10.6}$$

$$\lim_{t \to \infty} \text{Var}(H(t)) = \frac{\sigma^2}{2\theta} \tag{10.7}$$

To apply Equation 10.2 to generating mean reverting macroeconomic scenarios, the parameters θ, μ, and σ must be estimated from the history of the macroeconomic factor. μ is simply the long-run average. σ may be determined from the average through-the-cycle volatility σ_{TTC}^2 as

$$\sigma^2 = \frac{4}{3}\ln(2)\sigma_{TTC}^2 \tag{10.8}$$

θ may be derived from the half-life $t_{1/2}$, which is half the time needed for the current value to relax onto the long-run-average.

$$\theta = \frac{\ln(2)}{t_{1/2}} \tag{10.9}$$

10.2 Second-order Ornstein-Uhlenbeck

Although fairly simple, the Ornstein-Uhlenbeck process described above usually has a discontinuity in the rate of change. A graph of the scenario will always look unrealistic because of the sudden change in direction at the start of the scenario. Momentum can be included in the scenario generation by using a second-order Ornstein-Uhlenbeck process. The following provides a derivation of the necessary formulas.

We consider x_t as the solution of the following second order Ornstein-Uhlenbeck equation

$$dx_t = (\theta(\mu - x_t) + v_t)dt \qquad (10.10)$$
$$dv_t = -\theta_1 v_t dt + \sigma dw_t \qquad (10.11)$$

where x_t is the time series, μ is the long-run mean, σ is the volatility coefficient, w_t is a Wiener process, and θ, θ_1 are positive constants ($\theta \neq \theta_1$). The solution to Equations 10.10 & 10.11 is

$$x_t = \mu + C_1 e^{-\theta t} + C_2 e^{-\theta_1 t} + \frac{\sigma}{(\theta - \theta_1)} \int_0^t \left(e^{-\theta_1(t-\tau)} - e^{-\theta(t-\tau)} \right) dw_\tau \qquad (10.12)$$

where C_1, C_2 are arbitrary constants depending upon the initial conditions of x_t, v_t. The mean and variance of x_t are calculated as:

$$E(x_t) = \mu + C_1 e^{-\theta t} + C_2 e^{-\theta_1 t} \qquad (10.13)$$

where $E(x_t) \to \mu$ as $t \to \infty$.

$$\text{Var}(x_t) = \frac{\sigma^2}{2\theta_1(\theta + \theta_1)} \frac{1 - \left((\theta e^{-\theta_1 t} - \theta_1 e^{-\theta t})^2 + \theta\theta_1(e^{-\theta_1 t} - e^{-\theta t})^2 \right)}{(\theta - \theta_1)^2}$$

$$(10.14)$$

where $\text{Var}(x_t) \to \sigma^2/(\theta\theta_1(\theta + \theta_1))$ as $t \to \infty$. The time series up to the beginning of mean-reversion can be called y_t. This could include actual history and given scenario. The mean reverting process x_t begins at t_0. The goal is to obtain an extrapolation of y_t after time $t_0 = n$ as a mean-reverting 2D Ornstein-Uhlenbeck process with a smooth extrapolation of y_t for $t > t_0$. The best estimate of x_t is

$$\hat{x}_t = \mu + C_1 e^{-\theta t} + C_2 e^{-\theta_1 t} \qquad (10.15)$$

Therefore,

$$\hat{x}_n = \mu + C_1 e^{-\theta n} + C_2 e^{-\theta_1 n} = y_n, (7) \qquad (10.16)$$
$$\hat{x}_n - \hat{x}_{n-1} = C_1 \left(e^{-\theta n} - e^{-\theta(n-1)} \right) + C_2 \left(e^{-\theta_1 n} - e^{-\theta_1(n-1)} \right) \qquad (10.17)$$
$$\hat{x}_n - \hat{x}_{n-1} = y_n - y_{n-1}.(8) \qquad (10.18)$$

Solving this system produces

$$C_2 = (y_{n-1} - \mu - (y_n - \mu)e^\theta) / \left(e^{-\theta_1 n}(e^{\theta_1} - e^\theta)\right) \qquad (10.19)$$

$$C_1 = (y_n - \mu)e^{\theta n} - C_2 e^{(\theta - \theta_1)n} \qquad (10.20)$$

Values C_1, C_2 given in Equations 10.19 & 10.20 are substituted into Equation 10.15. For convenience and to avoid operations with big numbers $t_0 = n = 0$ was used.

Parameters μ and σ were obtained from the mean value and standard deviation of time series yt. Parameters θ, θ_1 are free and are set with the help of an optimization criterion (one of this criterion is similarity of Ornstein-Uhlenbeck process x_t to the time series yt at time $t \in [t_0 - \delta, t_0]$ for some given $\delta > 0$).

In the current study, values near $\theta = 3$, $\theta_1 = 4$ were usually obtained for extrapolating the macroeconomic factors. In that case

$$\hat{x}_t = \mu + C_1 e^{-\theta t} + C_2 e^{-\theta_1 t} \approx \mu + C_1 e^{-\theta t} \qquad (10.21)$$

for large t.

11

Dynamics of Loans

Models rarely fail because of what they include. They fail because of what they do not include. Before a model is estimated or validated, an analyst can know what will cause that model to fail simply by listing all the things that drive loan performance and recognizing that failure comes when an unmodeled driver of performance changes rapidly and unexpectedly. Of course, no model can capture everything, but by knowing what is not included, the analyst can know when and where to check for weaknesses.

11.1 Modeling Distributions

Predicting future losses is a portfolio question. Intrinsically, the question is not about whether one account has stopped paying and another still is. To predict portfolio losses, overall trends are most important. Figure 11.1 is a visualization of the risk of default for loans in a portfolio at different slices in time. From one time interval to the next, individual accounts may shift above and below the median of the distribution of risk, but total loss reserves will change only from systematic changes in the distribution. Although being able to answer which are the highest risk accounts is of high value for management, for loss forecasting one needs to identify the drivers of the median.

The distinction between movements of individual accounts and movements of the overall distribution can be described as information odds and population odds. For probability of default or attrition, the natural and most common approach is to create a model of the log odds. A model $s(x)$ that predicts log-odds of default given some information

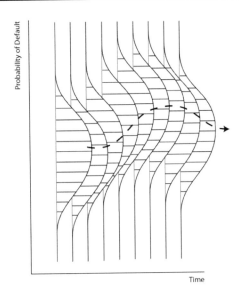

Figure 11.1. A visualization of how the distribution of accounts will shift in probability of default over time as the macroeconomic environment changes with the dashed line representing the median of the distribution. For an accurate total default forecast, we do not need to track this for individual accounts or even for small segments. Capturing overall shifts in the distribution is sufficient.

x is related tot he probability of default as

$$p(x) = \frac{1}{1 + e^{-s(x)}} \tag{11.1}$$

Following Thomas (Thomas et al. 2002) and using Bayes' Theorem, that model of log-odds can be expressed as

$$s(x) = \ln o(G|x) = \ln \left(\frac{p_G f(x \mid G)}{p_B f(x \mid B)} \right) =$$
$$\ln \left(\frac{p_G}{p_B} \right) + \ln \left(\frac{f(x \mid G)}{f(x \mid B)} \right) \tag{11.2}$$

or

$$s(x) = \ln o_{Pop} + \ln o_{Inf} \tag{11.3}$$

where o_{Pop} is the population odds and o_{Inf} is the information odds. Therefore, the population odds is the mean of the distribution in Figure 11.1 and the information odds capture the loan-level, idiosyncratic variations about the mean. As shown in the picture, the populations odds can change with time and will have different drivers from the information odds.

11.2 Performance Dynamics

In the context of retail lending such as the mortgages modeled in this study, the following items may impact performance.

1. **Origination:** Consumer & loan information.

2. **Vintages:** Biases for specific cohorts.

3. **Lifecycle:** Changes with age of the loan.

4. **Behavior:** As the loan matures, observed loan performance can refine the predictions.

5. **Account management:** Changes made to individual loans.

6. **Environment:** Changes in the economy or portfolio management.

From this list, the Lifecycle and Environment can be thoughts of as causing changes in the population odds, whereas Origination and Account management impact the information odds. Behavioral information such as recent delinquency is difficult to categorize, because it is also driven by factors that impact both the population and information odds.

The following graphs successively add the information components in the list above to a hypothetical account(s) to illustrate the causes of the observed risk. Figure 11.2 starts with a single hypothetical account that originates at some point in time and defaults at some future date.

Figure 11.2. A loan is originated (red dot), performs for some time (red line), and then terminates (red X).

Figure 11.3 adds origination information. Based upon what was known at origination, the eventual default was not a surprised. A non-zero probability of default always existed.

Figure 11.3. The probability of default is not uniform for all loans, so PD models try to measure this scaling.

Figure 11.4 shows that many accounts are originated at the same time, a vintage, and that the accounts in a vintage may have a unique additional risk that is not captured by the information available at origination. Vintage-specific information could be measurable items, like changes in marketing or underwriting. More often it is some form of adverse selection.

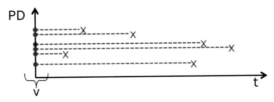

Figure 11.4. Many accounts may be originated at the same time period, referred to as a vintage. A vintage can have unique risk compared to other vintages.

Adverse selection is where the pool of applicants shifts relative to historic norms. A lender's underwriting criteria might not have changed, but the applicant pool may shift in ways that are not visible to the underwriting process. The traditional example of adverse selection is where a lender's offered loan interest rate is outside the current market range. If that rate is significantly higher than the competitors' rates, then only the most desperate borrowers will apply.

Microeconomic adverse selection refers to times when economic conditions look unfavorable for borrowing, so conservative consumers stay out of the market, leaving only the risk-taking consumers (Breeden and Canals-Cerdá 2016).

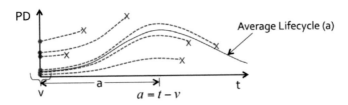

Figure 11.5. The probability of defaulting is not uniform through the life of a loan. This incorporates the loss timing in the PD estimate.

Figure 11.5 adds the risk associated with the lifecycle versus age of the loan. The lifecycle is a nonlinear function that is unique to the specific product offered.

If the forecast is being created from a starting point after the origination date, the intervening models provide additional information, behavioral information, that provides further adjustment to the default risk of the accounts, Figure 11.6.

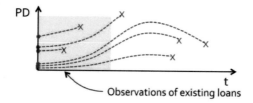

Figure 11.6. As the behavior of a loan is observed, this modifies our expectation of the probability of default.

Figure 11.7 returns to a single account to illustrate the impacts of account management. In this case, the affect of a credit line increase is shown in the blue line. Initially a line increase provides more financial flexibility to the borrower, so the probability of default decreases. However, as the additional credit is used, the default risk increases above the previous level.

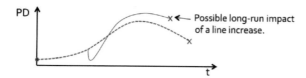

Figure 11.7. Account management can change the default risk of a loan through time.

Lastly, Figure 11.8 adds the environmental effects, economics and seasonality, to produce the final variation in default risk.

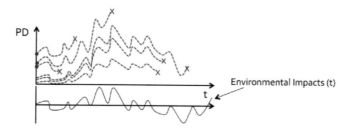

Figure 11.8. The external environment impacts the default probability of all active loans.

If we know that all these items drive default, then all models can be seen as a compromise, attempting to include as much of the known structure as possible given the available data.

12

Why Models Fail

From experience, models seem to fail for one of two reasons:

1. Omission: Not including necessary structure in the model
2. Colinearity: Not estimating the assumed structures correctly

The purpose of the previous chapter was to review structure that may drive the performance of the loans. Major failures almost always come because of something not captured in the models. For the 2009 US Mortgage Crisis, most forecasting failures came because lenders were using roll rate models. Those model assumed no change in vintage quality or lifecycle effects until they could be indirectly observed through rising delinquency. By then, it was too late.

To predict future model failures, look for what is left out. Early warning monitoring should be established for those conditions that the models do not include, so that management will know when not to trust the model. This is already standard practice in scorecards, where score-to-odds charts are tracked, looking for times when the score will be weak and should be rebuilt.

The other major category of failure comes during estimation, where the estimates incorrectly assign the structure in the data. For example, a model that includes both delinquency and economic factors may have difficulty in attributing what delinquency is due to intrinsic behavior of the consumer and what is due indirectly to the economic factors. The colinearity between delinquency and economics may be resolved in-sample, but for scenario-based forecasting, any colinearity with macroeconomic scenarios can confuse or dilute the macroeconomic impacts. Just because an estimator provides unique coefficients in-sample does not mean those coefficients will be correct for scenario-based forecasting.

12.1 Multicolinearity

The colinearity problem can appear in very different forms depending upon the type of model used and yet still have the same root cause. As discussed in Section 6.2, Age-Period-Cohort models make the colinearity explicit as a specification error in allocating the linear trend between the age, vintage, and time functions. The nonlinear structure along those dimensions is unique, so only the linear trends are ambiguous.

Recent work (Breeden et al. 2015) has connected the linear trend ambiguity in APC models with a colinearity problem in Cox proportional hazards models. When explicit factors are used instead of nonparametric functions, the specification error is resolved, but is replaced with a colinearity problem of equal magnitude. If the Cox PH model uses only factors along the vintage or time dimensions, then the colinearity is exactly the same as in the APC model.

For any of these models, when cross-terms are added between the three dimensions, the colinearity problems extend beyond the linear trends to the nonlinear structure as well. Using delinquency as input to a model is the greatest challenge, because it is also predictable from functions of age, vintage, and time.

For both specification errors and colinearity, estimators exist that provide unique solutions. The problem is that a unique solution in-sample does not guarantee accurate forecasts out of sample. The assumptions made to resolve the linear trend specification error can fit the data well in-sample, but may result in strong drift out-of-sample. In exactly the same way, resolving colinearity in-sample may still result in strong trends out-of-sample when the forecasts are driven with macroeconomic or new origination scenarios.

The only practical solution to the linear trend and colinearity problems is long term extrapolation. Banking regulations are built on an assumption that performance is stationary over time. Talking about Through-the-cycle estimates is nonsensical unless one assumes that a long-term stable level exists. We actually know that business practices have trended through time with the introduction of new products and lending to new demographic segments. Therefore, it is the economic impact on loan performance that is being assumed to be stable over long periods.

One need not accept these regulatory through-the-cycle assumptions as true, but if models are being built for regulatory purposes, then those models must capture these assumptions. Therefore, a forecast or backcast over many years should produce a steady-state response if steady-state assumptions are made about economics and originations. It does not prove that the underlying model coefficients are correct—only that the colinearity that we know to be present has not impaired the model to the point of violating fundamental assumptions.

The back-casting method has been used before to explicitly solve for the appropriate trends in APC models (Breeden and Thomas 2016). For factor-based models practitioners tend to swap factors in and out until a stable trend is achieved. The justification is always around reducing colinearity, but the practical truth is that it is a manual, hit-or-miss approach to getting the extrapolation correct.

12.2 Modeling the Data or the System

Some key model design decisions actual come down to a philosophical question.

"Are we modeling the data or the system?"

Almost without fail, statistics texts assume that a given dataset captures all that is known about a problem and techniques are provided to create models from that data. Taken to its extreme, this leads to data mining techniques that attempt to tease novel insight from the data alone with minimal structural assumptions.

Conversely, the data available for model development in lending is incredibly short. A large lender may have millions of accounts, making the data miners rejoice, but that data typically spans one economic cycle or less. To be clear, building models that use economic factors on one economic cycle or less is statistically invalid. From a rigorous statistical perspective, 99% of all stress test models developed by lenders are invalid. The estimates created in-sample are a fit to a single cycle which cannot really be validated or expected to perform well out-of-sample. When we are being honest over a beer in the pub, we admit to one another that these are order-of-magnitude only.

What then should be made of requests to test the data to see if it is stationary? Most portfolios we are asked to analyze today do not have data back to the peak of the previous cycle, roughly 2003. The worst may only have data back to 2011, for example. As discussed in Section 4.1, unit root tests applied to the specific data available can give completely different answers from what would be obtained from a longer dataset.

We can look to specific datasets like the Fannie Mae and Freddie Mac data and see that PDs are stationary when observed long enough. Cointegration between default rates and unemployment only tests positive when tested on short segments of the data. Many validators and examiners take a textbook approach of testing just the available data. Such tests might lead one to conclude that first differences of a short time series should be modeled instead of levels, e.g. that the change in a default rate or roll rate should be modeled instead of the rate itself. However, modeling changes emphasizes a different kind of structure. Monthly changes in default rates or roll rates are dominated by collections policies and account management. Instead, if levels are modeled, the dominant structure will be macroeconomic drivers.

Based upon experiences such as these, we have taken the philosophical position that the system should be modeled, not the data. We know from decades of data that the US unemployment rate series is stationary. Regulation implies and we agree that macroeconomic impacts on default rates (the environment functions from APC models) are stationary. Therefore, decisions on using differences or changes were made in this study based upon what is known about loan portfolios over the long run, rather than this one piece of data.

A similar question arises with including autoregressive terms in the model estimation. Including autoregressive terms is not a matter of statistical interpretation the way unit-root tests can be. The problem with including them derives from the physics of the problem. When the goal is to build a model that predicts future losses from macroeconomic changes, invariably the residuals will be autocorrelated because of the things that are unknown. The current dataset provides no information on changes in collections policies, which would clearly impact delinquency and default. Some of these changes were adopted simultaneously across the industry in response to the recession, so diversification across portfolios cannot be assumed to solve the problem. Standard econometric modeling practice suggests that autoregressive (AR) or moving average (MA) terms should be included to correct the model for the missing factors. These AR and MA terms are an attempt to capture unmodeled structure in the forecasts – primarily variations in portfolio composition. Out of sample, these models are used for multi-period extrapolation. They will not have any input from real portfolio performance to guide the error-correcting aspect of these terms. Therefore, the AR term will create a feedback loop serving to amplify the factors that are explicitly present in the model, namely macroeconomic factors. When measured in-sample, AR terms are most likely capturing credit risk variation, account aging, and management actions. Out-of-sample, they amplify the macroeconomic contribution, which should have already been properly captured with the assigned coefficients. In general, autoregressive terms are not appropriate in a multi-period model using macroeconomic factors, as they serve primarily to destabilize the result.

Excluding autoregressive terms does mean that serial correlation will persist in the residuals. The estimated coefficients will be optimized, but the standard p-values will overestimate the quality of the result. To estimate the p-values correctly, one needs simply to employ a robust estimator such as the Newey-West estimator.

MA terms that would extrapolate residual errors one step forward in-sample are then undefined for a multi-step forecast. How far and via which process the MA terms should be extrapolated into the future is not known from theory and generally not robust when estimated in-sample. For these reasons, no MA terms were included in these models.

13

Model Convergence

First there was Basel II, with its subsequent years of interpretation, model development, review, documentation, and refinement. In retrospect, it's surprising how much effort went into estimating 12-month forward default rates under an average economic scenario.

Then came stress testing. CCAR (Comprehensive Capital Analysis and Review) and DFAST (Dodd-Frank Act Stress Testing) required banks to look further into the future (9 quarters) under alternate economic scenarios. This is a fundamentally more challenging task than Basel II, because one must quantify and incorporate economic sensitivities, adjust for attrition / pay-off, and quantify not just the probability of default, but also the timing of default.

As always happens with new regulations, lenders and regulators both evolve their knowledge and expectations of what should be considered standard practice. For CCAR, lenders consistently report that the Federal Reserve examiners want the best possible models and at the loan-level. However, for the banks with assets less than \$50 billion but greater than \$10 billion that must only comply with DFAST, loan-level models are not emphasized. Some examiners are reported to have made comments such as, "If you build a more complex model, you will receive increased scrutiny." Thus, the path of least resistance for banks has been to create simple time series models for DFAST (of the type demonstrated here), even though such models fail to capture key portfolio dynamics and do not prepare banks for crossing the CCAR threshold.

Now we have CECL (the Financial Accounting Standards Board's rules for Current Expected Credit Loss) and IFRS 9 (the International Accounting Standards Board's rules for International Financial Reporting Standards, latest revision), and both banks and examiners are groaning.

Please, not another parallel model with different requirements and another cycle of interpretation, development, review, documentation, and refinement! The following sections provide a quick review of common modeling practices for the different regulations. We will start with what is, before we look to what could be.

13.1 Basel II

Although subsequent rules have been adopted to add to the initial calculation, Basel II continues to encapsulate the methodology for computing credit risk capital. Measuring regulatory capital is an exercise in quantifying the unknowable. We cannot know what a once-in-a-thousand-year event looks like, but we know how that calculation should scale with the risk of the borrower and across products. Starting from some additional assumptions, Basel II provides a formula for the distribution of possible losses that can be scaled with a few input parameters. The task for lenders is to compute the probability of default (PD) for the next 12 months as an input to the formula.

The PD calculation is intended to be a through-the-cycle PD, meaning that it corresponds to the expected performance of the current portfolio in an "average" economic environment. Initial efforts took this to mean that an average of historic PD levels for the portfolio would be sufficient, but this failed dramatically because of the changing credit risk profile of loan portfolios through the economic cycle. Today, best practice is to make a forecast of the next 12-month PD for the specific loans on the books today, compensating for recent performance, age of the loans, and a scenario for an average (through-the-cycle) economic environment. Notably, Basel II does not require a forecast of when the future losses will occur, only the cumulative risk. Therefore, Basel II PD models tend to look more like traditional scores without explicit treatment of attrition or loss timing.

13.2 CCAR

In the 2009 Global Financial Crisis and concurrent US Mortgage Crisis, we must admit that Basel II did not perform very well. Either that or accept that 2009 was worse than a once-in-a-thousand year event. Unlikely. CCAR is a direct response to the shortcomings of Basel II. One OCC senior analyst gave a presentation where he demonstrated that the Basel II formula did not come close to fitting the in-sample data. His concluding remark for his talk was, "Don't trust the formula. Don't trust the result." Rather than employing a specific formula for which we know the starting assumptions are not met (at least for retail loans), banks are instructed to build their own models to predict portfolio performance under a specific set of macroeconomic scenarios.

Because CCAR models must incorporate specific macroeconomic scenarios and predict 27 months into the future, two things immediately change relative to Basel II. The forecasts must be monthly or quarterly and the models must capture the competing risks of default and attrition / pay-off. This means that CCAR models are not scores. We must start from a time series perspective, but they cannot be simple time series models either. Particularly for retail loans and deposits, the changing risk with the age of the loan can confound simple time series models. In other words, a simple time series model will only work if the portfolio is static in all respects other than macroeconomic drivers. It must be unchanging in terms of the credit risk of new loans, the loan inflow volume must match the outflow, and the portfolio must be practically unmanaged in any sense that would impact account performance. None of these are ever true for a real-life portfolio.

Therefore, more sophisticated models have evolved as standard CCAR practice. CCAR examiners have expressed a clear preference for loan-level models, although as this study shows, loan-level models will not necessarily provide greater accuracy. State transition models and survival models as described here are two of the common approaches.

13.3 DFAST

For the smaller but still significant lenders, DFAST is the minimum stress testing requirement. The task for the modeler is no different from CCAR, i.e. build a long-range loss forecasting model that incorporates the same macroeconomic scenarios as CCAR. At this lowest level, none of the requirements have changed, so we would expect that DFAST models would be similar to CCAR models. However, with the intent of making things easier for smaller institutions, DFAST examiners have not pushed for the same model sophistication as CCAR examiners.

Although simple time series models have been most common, whenever lenders move beyond those methods, the preferred approaches will be the same as those described for CCAR, though probably with less emphasis on loan-level modeling.

13.4 IFRS 9

As discussed in Section 2.9, IFRS 9 is the new international accounting standard for estimating loan loss reserves that shares much in common with CECL. Unlike previous standards, IFRS 9 requires a forward-looking estimate of losses. How the losses are estimated depends upon the performance of the loan. Three stages are recognized as shown below.

Stage 1: Performing loans – 12-month loss forecast

Stage 2: Significantly increased risk and not low risk – Lifetime loss forecast

Stage 3: Impaired loans – Lifetime loss forecast

One could naturally perform all of the above analysis at the loan-level, making individual assessments of increased credit risk. However, the IFRS 9 guidelines specifically state that pooled analysis may be necessary to identify the increased risk of an individual loan—risk by association. As seen in the US Mortgage Crisis , an account may be in a vintage and segment that is experiencing much higher than expected losses. Although that account may not yet be exhibiting stress, through membership in that specific vintage / segment the account may warrant Stage 2 loss estimation.

Because of this support of pooled analysis and the need for lifetime loss estimation from any account age through to the end of term or foreseeable future, vintage models have rapidly become the standard for IFRS 9 loss estimation for retail loans. In Europe, the standard approach is referred to as EMV modeling (Exogenous-Maturation-Vintage). EMV models are a direct descendant of Dual-time Dynamics (Breeden 2007), which is in turn largely equivalent to Age-Period-Cohort models. All these vintage analysis methods decompose the historic performance into functions of age, vintage, and time.

These vintage models may serve as the forecast for Stage 1 and to provide the benchmark against which Stage 2 transition is judged. When accounts are assigned to Stage 2, they will be higher risk than the vintage or segment from which they are drawn and therefore some additional risk scaling will be necessary to apply to the original vintage forecast. Alternately, a loan-level model may be used to assess the lifetime expected loss for the Stage 2 accounts.

Loan-level modeling is an attractive option for IFRS 9 because of the intuitive desire to isolate those accounts that are causing the increased risk. However, since the IFRS 9 guidelines specifically comment on the need to set higher reserves even for accounts that do not currently show risk but are associated with other accounts that do, we need a definition for Stage 2 that is more expansive than a simple delinquency trigger. For a loan-level definition of Stage 2 increased risk, looking beyond delinquency we could also consider utilization (for lines-of-credit), credit bureau scores, debt-to-income, loan-to-value (for auto or mortgage), etc. Therefore, a loan-level model can be created to incorporate these factors, but it should also incorporate lifecycle effects in order to provide lifetime loss estimates, economic factors, and residual vintage risk beyond the score. Also, we need to capture the attrition probability so that the lifetime estimates are correct.

For retail lending, the above can be achieved with Cox proportional hazards models or a panel model that takes lifecycle and environment as inputs. The loan-level model would not need to be used for the Stage 1 loss forecast, but only to assess when the loan's credit risk has exceeded a predetermined bound. Then the loan-level model could be used to assess the lifetime loss.

State transition models can also be used to fulfill the needs of IFRS 9. Although in practice they tend not to strongly model the lifecycle effect, this can be incorporated in most cases.

For commercial lending, lifecycles are generally unimportant, so state transition or panel models are most common, both of which are usually created at the loan-level. For line-of-credit products, IFRS 9 includes risk associated with future purchases through the life of the loan.

Considering all of these details, IFRS 9 and CCAR results could well be created on the same underlying models, with some adjustments for different philosophies on conservatism, new originations, and unused credit lines.

13.5 Comparing Regulations

How do we bring unity to such differing requirements? With a few nudges, it's quite possible. Basel II and DFAST are the outliers. If we start from Basel models, Table 13.1, the gap to CCAR or CECL / IFRS 9 is quite wide. A 12-month average Basel PD could be viewed as an input to a more complete model, but the simplest approach is to start from CCAR or CECL / IFRS 9. To satisfy Basel, one need only use a through-the-cycle economic scenario and aggregate the first 12-months of the forecast. However, early indications are that Basel IV will largely do away with the advanced IRB (internal ratings-based) approach, instead using just the standardized approach. If so, Basel IV will no longer use a model and be cut from the list.

CECL and IFRS 9 modeling needs actually come closest to CCAR, so long as modelers ignore the line-of-credit paradox for CECL. Lenders of all sizes and business models, if they want models that are defendable to auditors and examiners, will need models with economic sensitivity, competing risks of attrition and default, and monthly or quarterly forecasting through the life of the loan. The best models will be loan-level so that they consider current loan conditions and integrate with accounting systems.

Task	Common practice
Basel II	12-month average PDs, worst-case EAD and LGD
CCAR	State transition and survival models
DFAST	Commonly use time series
IFRS 9	Vintage / survival models
CECL	Anything but time series models, as long as it considers economics and loss timing

Table 13.1. Summary of standard practice for modeling.

Clearly, a large bank building a CCAR-compliant model can use the same model for DFAST, but if one starts with the commonly-built DFAST default rate time series models, life is not easy. A simple default rate time series model will not work for CECL or IFRS 9, because it does not capture any lifetime loss aspects. If two time series models are created for default and attrition, then they could be used to run off existing loan balances through the life of the loan as demonstrated here, but not with much accuracy. For DFAST lenders that are not large enough for CCAR, satisfying CECL or IFRS 9 may push them to create CCAR-class models anyway, and their DFAST submissions will be much better because of it.

Thinking through the similarities and differences between all these requirements leads us to the follow commonalities.

- Economic sensitivity (to model different economic scenarios)
- Monthly or quarterly forecasting (to incorporate economic scenarios)
- Competing risks of default and attrition / pay-off (for long-range forecasting)
- Lifecycles in loss and attrition / pay-off timing (for long-range forecasting)

- Loan-level (for CCAR and best-practice CECL / IFRS 9 and Basel)

In most general terms, two primary classes of model can satisfy these needs: state transition models and survival models. For decades, lending analytics were little more than credit scores and moving average roll rate models, but neither of these methods was forward-looking. Notable, all mortgage lenders prior to the US Mortgage Crisis had both roll rates and credit scores. Of course, few claim to have predicted the collapse in house prices, but the increased default rates due to higher risk loans and the timing of those losses were quite predictable. In fact, simple vintage models performed quite well through the mortgage crisis. With the failure of moving average methods made blatantly clear, all areas of regulation are moving to forward-looking methods.

Although the transition can be painful, one wonders how we can function without these. How can loans be priced without knowing the expected lifetime losses? If profits are large and competitors are few, then portfolio management can be passive and models are not necessary. That business environment has not existed in lending since about the 1980's. To survive today, these models are needed throughout the organization. Model convergence is just making sure that we create good models across the range.

References

Bangia, A., Diebold, F. X., Kronimus, A., Schagen, C., and Schuermann, T. (2002). Ratings migration and the business cycle, with application to credit portfolio stress testing. *Journal of Banking & Finance*, 26(2):445 – 474.

Bennett, D. E. (2017). Governance and organizational requirements for effective model risk management. *Journal of Risk Model Validation*, 11(4):97–116.

Berteloot, K., Verbeke, W., Castermans, G., Van Gestel, T., Martens, D., and Baesens, B. (2013). A novel credit rating migration approach using macroeconomic indicators. *Journal of Forecasting*, 32:654–672.

Breeden, J. L. (2007). Modeling data with multiple time dimensions. *Computational Statistics & Data Analysis*, 51:4761 – 4785.

Breeden, J. L. (2010). Testing retail lending models for missing cross-terms. *Journal of Risk Model Validation*, 4(4).

Breeden, J. L. (2014). *Reinventing Retail Lending Analytics: Forecasting, Stress Testing, Capital and Scoring for a World of Crises, 2nd Impression.* Risk Books, London.

Breeden, J. L. (2016). Incorporating lifecycle and environment in loan-level forecasts and stress tests. *European Journal of Operational Research*, 255(2):649 – 658.

Breeden, J. L. (2017a). The deep future analytics cecl study: Alternatives, impacts, accuracy, and complexity. Technical report, Deep Future Analytics.

Breeden, J. L. (2017b). One model to rule them all. *RMA Journal*, 4:28–33.

Breeden, J. L., Bellotti, A., and Yablonski, A. (2015). Instabilities using cox ph for forecasting or stress testing loan portfolios. In *Credit Scoring and Credit Control XIV Conference*, Edinburgh.

Breeden, J. L. and Canals-Cerdá, J. J. (2016). Consumer risk appetite, the credit cycle, and the housing bubble. *Working Papers, Research Department, Federal Reserve Bank of Philadelphia*.

Breeden, J. L. and Liang, S. (2015). A mean-reverting model to create macroeconomic scenarios for credit risk models. *Journal of Risk Model Validation*, 9(4):1–12.

Breeden, J. L. and Thomas, L. C. (2008). The relationship between default and economic cycle for retail portfolios across countries: identifying the drivers of economic downturn. *Journal of Risk Model Validation*, 2(3):11 – 44.

Breeden, J. L. and Thomas, L. C. (2016). Solutions to specification errors in stress testing models. pages 830–840.

Breeden, J. L., Thomas, L. C., and McDonald III, J. (2008). Stress testing retail loan portfolios with dual-time dynamics. *Journal of Risk Model Validation*, 2(2):43 – 62.

Breusch, T. S. (1978). Testing for autocorrelation in dynamic linear models. *Australian Economic Papers*, 17:334 – 355.

Cox, D. R. (1972). Regression models and life-tables. *Journal of the Royal Statistical Society. Series B (Methodological)*, 34(2):187–220.

Cox, D. R. and Oakes, D. O. (1984). *Analysis of Survival Data*. Chapman and Hall, London.

Durbin, J. and Watson, G. S. (1950). Testing for serial correlation in least squares regression, i. *Biometrika*, 37(3-4):409–428.

Durbin, J. and Watson, G. S. (1951). Testing for serial correlation in least squares regression, ii. *Biometrika*, 38(1-2):159–179.

FASB (2016). Measurement of credit losses on financial instruments. Technical Report No. 2016-13, Financial Accounting Standards Boardt.

FDIC. FDIC quarterly banking profile. `http://www.fdic.gov/bank/analytical/qbp`. Accessed: 2017.

FDIC (2017). Adoption of supervisory guidance on model risk management. Technical report, Federal Deposit Insurance Corporation.

FRB (2011). Supervisory guidance on model risk management. Technical report, Board of Governors of the Federal Reserve System.

Glenn, N. D. (2005). *Cohort Analysis, 2nd Edition*. Sage, London.

Godfrey, L. G. (1978). Testing against general autoregressive and moving average error models when the regressors include lagged dependent variables. *Econometrica*, 46:1293 – 1301.

Goldman, A. I. (1992). Eventcharts: Visualizing survival and other timed-events data. *American Statistician*, 46:13–18.

Gujarati, D. N. and Porter, D. C. (2009). *Basic Econometrics*. McGraw-Hill Irwin, Boston, 5th edition.

Holford, T. R. (1983). The estimation of age, period and cohort effects for vital rates. *Biometrics*, 39(2):311–324.

IASB (2014). IFRS 9 financial instruments. Technical report, IFRS Foundation.

Israel, R., Rosenthal, J., and Wei, J. (2000). Finding generators for markov chains via empirical transition matrices, with application to credit ratings. *Mathematical Finance*, 11:245–265.

Judge, G., Griffiths, W. E., Hill, R. C., Lütkepohl, H., and Lee, T.-C. (1985). *The Theory and Practice of Econometrics*. Wiley Publ.

Keiding, N. (1990). Statistical inference in the lexis diagram. *Philosophical Transactions of the Royal Society of London A: Mathematical, Physical and Engineering Sciences*, 332(1627):487–509.

Keyfitz, N. (1968). *Introduction to the Mathematics of Population*. Addison-Wesley, Reading, Mass.

Lexis, W. (1875). *Einleitung in die Theorie der Bevölkerungsstatistik*. Karl J. Trübner, Strassburg.

Ljung, G. M. and Box, G. E. P. (1978). On a measure of a lack of fit in time series models. *Biometrika*, 65(2):297–303.

Mason, W. and Fienberg, S. (1985). *Cohort Analysis in Social Research: Beyond the Identification Problem*. Springer.

Moran, P. A. P. (1950). Notes on continuous stochastic phenomena. *Biometrika*, 37(1):17–23.

OCC (2011). Supervisory guidance on model risk management. Technical report, Office of the Comptroller of the Currency.

Reserve, F. (2013). Capital planning at large bank holding companies: Supervisory expectations and range of current practice. Technical report, Board of Governors of the Federal Reserve System, August, Washington.

Ryder, N. B. (1965). The cohort as a concept in the study of social change. *American Sociological Review*, 30(6):843–861.

Scandizzo, S. (2016). *The Validation of Risk Models: A Handbook for Practitioners*. Palgrave Macmillan, New York.

Schmid, V. and Held, L. (2007). Bayesian age-period-cohort modeling and prediction - bamp. *Journal of Statistical Software, Articles*, 21(8):1–15.

Taylor, J. (1999). *Monetary Policy Rules*, chapter A Historical Analysis of Monetary Policy Rules, pages 319–347. University of Chicago Press.

Thomas, L. C., Edelman, D. B., and Crook, J. N. (2002). *Credit Scoring and Its Applications*. Society for Industrial and Applied Mathematics, Philadelphia.

Thomas, L. C., Ho, J., and Scherer, W. T. (2001). Time will tell: behavioural scoring and the dynamics of consumer credit assessment. *IMA Journal of Management Mathematics*, 12(1):89–103.

Truck, S. (2014). Forecasting credit migrations matrices with business cycle effects p model comparison. *The European Journal of Finance*, pages 359–379.

Trudolyubov, S. and Breeden, J. L. (2011). Estimating the effects of adjustable rate mortgage resets. In *Credit Scoring and Credit Control XII Conference*, Edinburgh.

Uhlenbeck, G. E. and Ornstein, L. S. (1930). On the theory of brownian motion. *Physical Review*, 38:823 – 841.

Vandenschrick, C. (2001). The lexis diagram, a misnomer. *Demographic Research*, 4(3):97–124.

Wei, J. (2003). A multi-factor, credit migration model for sovereign and corporate debts. *Journal of International Money and Finance*, 22:709–735.

Index

88930376R10119

Made in the USA
Lexington, KY
20 May 2018